SEEING
GOD
IN EVERYTHING

SHAUN SAUNDERS

Published by Godzchild Publications
a division of Godzchild, Inc.
22 Halleck St., Newark, NJ 07104
www.godzchildproductions.net

Printed in the United States of America

Library of Congress Cataloging-in-Publications Data
Seeing God In Everything: Chronicles of a Worshipful Scribe/Shaun Saunders.
Includes bibliographical references and scriptural references.
ISBN 978-0-9840955-0-6 (pbk.)
1. Saunders, Shaun. 2. Christianity – Religious Aspects. 3. Modern Day Parables. 4. Self-Sight – Daily Living

2009930053

To every thing there is a season,
and a time to every purpose under the heaven:
Ecclesiastes 3:1

For by him were all things created, that are in heaven, and that are
in earth, visible and invisible... all things were created by him, and
for him:
Colossians 1:16

Offertory Prayer

Gracious Lord,

You are the Transcendent One, who entered the world and dwelt among us as Word; Word that is Spirit, and Word that is Life; Word that demonstrates true humanity; Word that inspires and Word that challenges; Word that heals, and Word that rebukes; Word that makes hungry and Word that feeds.

Our hearts come to these pages open for all those things above, and all those things below, that we might possess them in abundance, knowing that You desire for Your Word to dwell in us richly.

As we read, build us up where we are torn down; plant Your desires in the fallowed ground of our minds. Grant our desires for righteousness, satisfy our longing for truth.

As we read, establish our hearts in purity; challenge our motives with virtue; correct our theology in conversation, Supply us with wisdom that transforms.

As we read, relinquish self centeredness and replace it with compassion, cause the scales of carnality to fall from our eyes; the dumbness of indifference from our ears that Your Word may dwell in us richly.

Take these writings around the corner and across the globe for Your glory. We commend the labor of Shaun and Ana to birth this book to You, Holy One; You have trusted them to communicate Your Word, now infuse them with power that they may embody what they have written.

Now, thank You that the seed of the Word of God has already hit the womb of their imagination. They are impregnated with the next volume, double the anointing for Volume II, and make us ready to hear in yet another dimension of Your glory. Amen!

Rev. Boris M. Bayless

Foreword

❧_____☙

I'm nearsighted. On a clear, sunny day I couldn't make my own mother out if she was thirty feet away. Well, I'm exaggerating somewhat. But I do have to strain sometimes to make people out when they are a considerable distance from me. I have often mistaken friends and foes for someone else until they've gotten up close to me. I've even had people get angry with me 'cause they said I rudely ignored their gestured greetings. Don't take it personal; I didn't recognize whom you were. Of course, this would be alleviated if I wore my glasses. But I always seem to lose them and therefore don't bother to wear them. Besides, my myopia isn't that bad. I can function without them just fine.

But I've been wondering lately: how much better would my vision be if I actually wore my glasses? What would it be like if I could see everything clearly, without strain or misperception? What if I saw everything as it really is as opposed to the frustrating illusions that sometimes flash before my nearsighted eyes?

As you read through *Seeing God in Everything* you may ask these same questions about God and your reality. For many of us are spiritually nearsighted when it comes to God. It's hard to make God out when He seems distant, far away. And we strain the eyes of our understanding to perceive Him, only to recognize later that we inadvertently ignored His gestures of grace because we were too busy trying to discern if it was really God or not. Like the disciples on the ship at sea, when Jesus comes to us in those stormy life moments, we often confuse Him with a ghost. But if we were to enhance our spiritual eyes with a kind of second sight, we would be able to make out the shadowy figures in front of us, knowing that God is trying to get our attention so we can be transformed, empowered, and led further in our purpose.

My lil brother Shaun is a gifted writer and I guarantee this book of parables will help your spiritual eyesight. Think of this as the Good Doctor's divine prescription for your spiritual eyes. As you read through these pages, it will be like you are wearing a pair of godly glasses that enhance your vision and relieve the strain of trying to make out the images in front of you. As you move forward in life, this book will have had the great affect of helping you see God in places you previously thought unimaginable. You will see God in chain locks, in wrinkled shirts, unendorsed checks, and blown tires. You will see God where you least expected God to show up. And you will know that God is all around you, loving you, challenging you, making you into the wonderful vision of a life you were meant to be.

Shaun's book will be a gift to your sight. I promise you. Let his stories become your own and then reflect on how you too are starting to see God in unexpected places. As you read these parables, I pray that God will enlighten the eyes of your understanding so that you may truly see Him in everything, even when He's thirty feet away.

CJ Rhodes
Jackson, MS
Duke Divinity '09

Dedication

❦ _____ ❧

– To two of the most faithful servants I know,

Bishop Willie J. Hamilton and Pastor Hattie P. Hamilton.
(Pastors of the Holiness Pentecostal Church of Christ, Newark, NJ)

My pastors, my grandparents, my heroes…

I am able to write this book because of you.

"Dada," your testimony still amazes me. Having dropped out of school in the 7th grade, you are a walking Bible. You didn't know how to read and write very well, but God taught you His Word, and as a result, you have gifted us with the knowledge of verse-by-verse memorization and application. Thank you!

"Mama," you have inspired me to trust God and pray about everything. Your testimony is doubly amazing. You did not abort my mother while you were in high school, so you left school to have a child. And at the age of 57, you returned to high school and earned your diploma! (plus 15 college credits! Haha). More than that, you've listened to me, you've counseled me, and you read this book at least twenty times before anyone else did! Thank you for your wise instruction. Every time you said, "This chronicle was good," I knew God was pleased.

Bishop and Pastor, thank you for teaching me to appreciate the Word of God.

Thank you for training me to know the Word for myself. Thank you for being the best grandparents a boy could ever ask for. Fifty years of marriage and counting.

I vow to make you proud in Jesus' name.

Table of Contents

Introduction..1

Chronicles of A Worshipful Scribe
❧ Volume I ☙

Chronicles that *Expose*

Chronicle 1: Sleeping on the Job...7
Chronicle 2: Ironing a Shirt...20
Chronicle 3: Complaining on the Telephone............................47

Chronicles that *Examine*

Chronicle 4: Endorsing a Check...73
Chronicle 5: Opening a Gate..99
Chronicle 6: Arguing at the Dinner Table.............................116

Chronicles that *Encourage*

Chronicle 7: Reviewing my Savings Account Balance............139
Chronicle 8: Turning the Jump Rope......................................161

Chronicles that *Evangelize*

Chronicle 9: Witnessing the Death of a Squirrel...................185
Chronicle 10: Buying a Valentine's Day Card.......................203

Afterword...223
Acknowledgements..225

INTRODUCTION

AN INTRODUCTORY LETTER TO THE READER

*When Jesus taught, He didn't use huge words that no one understood.
Instead, He taught in parables and used everyday props to explain the Word
of God to everyday people. You won't find anything new in this book, really.
I'm just copying off of the Master's style.* —Shaun Saunders

DEAR READER,

You have heard that it has been said, "God isn't speaking." But I say, "We aren't seeing." God is speaking but we aren't hearing. And we aren't hearing because we aren't seeing. And we aren't seeing because we aren't praying; and we aren't praying because we don't really believe in God.

Oh yes, we come and go to church, but most of us don't truly see God in everything. Many of us don't even want to see God in everything. *Let's be honest about it.* We may allow God in after our pastor has preached a captivating sermon, or after a family circumstance has forced us to our knees, but most of us will go about our entire day spiritually unaware of God's life-giving messages to us. We live disconnected from our Life-Source, and this is dangerous and detrimental to our spiritual health. We wait and wait and wait for that heavenly light to come on before we open our eyes and look around for God's heavenly clues. But by that time, we have become so disoriented and detached that nothing God shows us makes much sense to us anymore.

Friends, God is speaking all around us, but like the skinny boy who wants muscles and doesn't work out, we must exercise our spiritual gifts in order to see spiritual results. *Seeing God in Everything* will help you to exercise your abs of understanding, expand your biceps of knowledge, and retrain your muscles of hearing and seeing. In other words, this book will help you to stretch your sight so that you can better understand who God is, how God speaks, and the many ways God chooses to reveal the Scriptures to us every day.

In the pages to come, you will encounter a variety of chronicles that *expose, examine, encourage,* and *evangelize.* These ten chronicles, all written at different times during my young adult life, were handpicked by God to help you recognize Him in your own life journey. Each time God spoke to me, He didn't always speak in traditional ways. Sometimes, God used an ordinary experience to convey an extraordinary message. Other times, God used an unfamiliar face to reveal God's familiar voice. The *exposure* chronicles reveal how God can use inanimate objects like a locked gate, an ironed shirt or a media newsflash to set us in order. The *examination* chronicles help us to, well, examine ourselves; but they do so by asking a series of questions like, "How do I deal with difficult people? and, "Is my life officially prepared for heaven's deposit?" The *encouragement* chronicles reveal to us the purpose behind some of the most tumultuous seasons of our lives, and in the end of this section is a dream that envisions God's church coming together. I pray you will share it with others. And finally, this book ends with two chronicles about *evangelism* because we take seriously the Great Commission found in Matthew 28:19: "Go ye therefore and teach all nations." We firmly believe that all Christians must evangelize and all Christians must live out what it means to be saved so that others might ask, "What must I do to be saved?"

So, think of this book like you would a puzzle. Chronicles of different sizes, analogies of different shapes and colors—some funny, some serious—that all teach us to see God in the hidden sermons of our lives. I often like to say that seeing God is not a self-help book. Rather, it is sight-help book; intended to heal the spiritually blind and offer a new bifocal prescription for the nearsighted and farsighted Christian. This is *not* a devotional memoir where good things about God make you feel like being a Christian, nor is it an academically organized set of chapters where every page is identical to the page before it. *Seeing God in Everything* is conversational yet complete, eclectic yet cohesive, creative yet faithful to God's Word and the lessons therein.

Comprised of mini stories and many Scripture references,

Seeing God will challenge you to think like Jesus and see like Jesus. We have highlighted hundreds of Scriptures that will bring clarity to you immediately or over time, but believe me when I say, every citation is important. So, please take advantage of the Scripture glossary. Use these verses as a springboard for personal study and consecration time with the Lord. Read these chronicles, yes, but above that, take a few moments to read the Word for yourself.

As a final point, each chronicle ends with questions and practical points written to help you incorporate the lessons God has shared with us. It is my hope that every word to follow will become more than a book of mixed metaphors and cute analogies. I hope your eyes are better trained to discern God's voice. I pray that someone's blinded eyes are opened and that God will become more visible to you everywhere, everyday, all day.

Remember friends, God is still speaking. Chapters of God's Word are still being written now. The life of God therefore is not coffined inside of a book. The stage play called "God's Will" is being performed in and through us. The Disciples were God's tape recorder. Moses was God's stenographer. Paul was God's speechwriter. And we are God's audio files. So speak up and write clearly or else the world won't hear what God is saying now! Don't be afraid of the new and the unprecedented. Instead, re-envision the old in fresh ways and be careful not to enslave yourself to the grip of comfortable space, outworn traditions and spoiled formula. So, go on and...

Flex those spiritual muscles.
Let God stretch you beyond your imagination.
Let the mind of Christ be in you.
Let the peace of God be with you.
Let the love of God flow out of you.
See God in Everything!

I LOVE YOU ALL!
SHAUN

CHRONICLES THAT *EXPOSE*

ೞ_____ఞ

SLEEPING ON THE JOB

Wake up and Don't Hit the Brakes

ભ_____ૹ

Another parable put he forth unto them, saying, the kingdom of heaven is likened unto a man which sowed good seed in his field: But while men slept, his enemy came and sowed tares among the wheat, and went his way.
Matthew 13:24-25

The residence halls at Seton Hall are very different from the halls at Duke University. At Duke, students can come and go at leisure. They bring visitors into the building without having to sign anyone in. It's a very open and welcoming environment. Seton Hall, on the other hand, feels like a military base. No one at Seton Hall (and I do mean no one) can enter the dorm without an identification card. There are student staff members posted at a barricade-looking desk whose job it is to swipe and buzz during the day. But, between the hours of midnight and 6 AM, there are professional swipers (not snipers, swipers!) hired to monitor hall activity and ensure our safety. These security guards aren't volunteers. Oh no! They are paid to swipe and buzz, and on occasion, they will page a higher authority in cases of emergency. Seems like an easy job, right? Wrong.

Sometimes, I would meander into the halls during the wee hours of the morning—of course I was coming from a midnight revival you see—and would encounter this sweetheart of a security guard sleeping on the job. She was compensated like all of the other attentive workers, but she was asleep half of the night! And I'm not just talking an occasional drift or nod. I mean, she would sleep sleep; like, give-me- a-pillow-and-ear-plugs sleep. Ironically, she was always frightened by my presence, but never so frightened that she would stay awake for the rest of the night. A few hours later, she would be asleep again. A few months later, unbeknownst to her, she would be out of a job.

SEEING GOD IN THE TERMINATED SWIPER

Believe it or not, this story resembles a familiar parable in the New Testament. Jesus tells it to His disciples one day when He decides to be more of a teaching tutor than a preoccupied professor. You see, a tutor will walk you through the steps that you don't fully comprehend until you get it. A busy and detached professor, however, will most times dish out the information, lecture non-stop for an hour, and test you on it the following week. Hmmm…is your pastor or spiritual leader more of a superstar professor or a hands-on tutor? I'll leave that question alone for now. But anyway, here it is. Matthew 13:24-25.[1]

Jesus begins, "the kingdom of heaven is likened unto a man which sowed good seed in his field; but while men slept, his enemy came and sowed tares among the wheat, and went his way." Jesus doesn't just tell a story about the sleeping swiper. He goes on to explain the parable in verse 37-39. He says, "he that soweth the good seed is the Son of man; the field is the world; the good seed are the children…the enemy who sowed them is the devil, the harvest is the end of the age." Essentially, He gives the disciples the answers to the test. 1 + 1 = 2. Men Asleep + Enemy=Major Problem. It's as simple as that. *Only a tutor who wants the student to understand will knowingly give away the answers to the test.* But like most clueless students, the disciples don't get it. So, Jesus schedules another tutoring session for them. This time, however, the disciples are the main characters.

CALLING ALL DISCIPLES TO SWIPE AND BUZZ!

Matthew 26:36,40 Then cometh Jesus with them unto a place called Gethsemane, and saith unto the disciples, Sit ye here, while I go and pray yonder. And he cometh unto the disciples, and findeth them asleep, and saith unto Peter, what, could ye not watch with me one hour?

Time: 13 chapters later. Location: Gethsemane. Welcome disciples and readers to Gethsemane's garden (Matthew 26:36).[2] Jesus tells the disciples, "Sit ye here, while I go and pray yonder." An hour later, He catches them sleeping on the job. What a shame! Jesus comes back and to His disappointment has to reprimand His friends: "Could you men not keep watch with me for one hour?" He asks (Matthew 26:40).[3] Then, He admonishes them with words that sound exactly like the parable in Matthew 13: "Watch and pray, that ye enter not into temptation: the spirit indeed is willing, but the flesh is weak." What was Christ trying to convey to them? What was the point of Him telling them a story first, and then showing them by example later? Well, there is a two-fold lesson at work here. First, Jesus is trying to teach them to "watch and pray." That's obvious. Second, Jesus is saying (without saying), "Don't fall asleep on the job!" That's implied. Jesus knows if they fall asleep, then the enemy will come in, sow tares in the field, and ultimately, their "residence halls" will go unprotected.

LESSON #1 WATCH AND PRAY

Matthew 26:41 Watch and pray, that ye enter not into temptation…

Let's chitchat a little about these two lessons. First, notice how Jesus never requires the disciples to do something that He isn't willing to do Himself. He is in the garden praying, but, on occasion, He takes off the "prayer hat" to check on His boys. He's *watching* and *praying*. Here's a quick nugget for the road: you will never reach people by preaching at them. You must learn to preach *with* them. Step away from the pulpit sometimes and just be as human as pastorally possibly. Learn from those you intend to impact and stop pretending that your bedroom is situated next to Gethsemane's garden. *O.K. Back to the lesson.* What is also interesting is that Jesus doesn't require them to meditate on the law while He's off praying somewhere; neither does He require them to lay hands on the sick and post-date all healing testimonies to Pentecost Sunday while He's away from the office. No. He just asks them to watch and pray. Two simple instructions. Swipe and Buzz, y'all…just swipe and buzz. But sadly, they can't even put two and two together.

Now, to me, it is no grand coincidence that Jesus invites these men to pray with Him. I mean, let's face it: Jesus is obsessed about this prayer thing. Every time He shows up missing in the Gospels, He's usually somewhere praying. So much so, He gives up food for weeks at a time to pray (Matthew 4:2).[4] Undoubtedly, Jesus is a praying man. The disciples know that about Him. What they don't know, however, is why Jesus tells them to watch while praying. What's up with the watch part, Jesus? In their minds, the best prayers are done with their eyes closed (which I still don't understand, but anyway); so, why does Jesus say watch and pray? What does sight have to do with one's prayer life? Simple answer: EVERYTHING. That's my answer, and I think Jesus might agree. Seeing God and praying to God has everything to do with understanding what God is trying to say to us, His children.

Now, let me change lanes for a second. Answer me this: what happens when you wake up? When you first open your eyes, what do you experience? First, your eyelids slightly crack open, right? Right. Then, you brush away the crust that has formed overnight around the corner of your eyes, and for just a few seconds, you can see but you can't *see*. *You know what I mean.* It's that hazy stage where you can notice the shape of a thing but can't make out the actual image; and it's not until your brain adjusts to the light that you are able to identify the alarm clock on the coffee table. Yes! What a wonderful feeling it is to realize the image you see in front of you in all of its intricate detail. In the same way, prayer opens up our spiritual eyes. This is a simple revelation, but an important one nonetheless. Prayer allows you to see things for what they truly are, and what you *see* has a lot to do with how open your eyes are to God's light of revelation. One translation of Matthew 26:41[5] says, "Keep watch with prayer" and that's interesting because, in my opinion, watching God move through our prayers is the best gift we could ever receive from Him. More than a material blessing, seeing God's hand in our lives is far more rewarding and relational. But the disciples couldn't see God move at all while they were sleeping, or, inattentive. They had to open their eyes and stare into the reality of God while praying for the clarity of God. That's what prayer means—to *speak* or to *communicate* as an *alert* vessel to the real God who hears you, even as you search out for more clarity in God, about God.

To put it differently, Jesus understood the connection between sight and spirit, and He used this real life event to teach a new way of thinking about prayer to a bunch of sleepy swipers (who were nearing termination), but they just didn't seem to get it. When Jesus tells them to watch and pray, He's exposing them to the power of spiritual sight. He's teaching them a simple lesson that actually undergirds this entire book's thesis. That is, the more you stare into the deadening darkness of temptation and distraction, the more likely you will see yourself darkly. But, the more you see God in the midst of your everyday life experiences, the more you will be exposed to God's heavenly view of things on earth. This is the power of attentive prayer in action. This is the kind of prayer that will enhance your vision and guide your insight. Thus, the man who does not pray cannot see. And the Christian who does not watch and pray is still a Christian, but a blind Christian at best. *Watch and Pray.* That's lesson number 1.

------------ ◈ ------------

People are sleepwalking around town, driving to work, or going to school and all the while, their spiritual eyes are shut. If they are not completely blind (you know if prayer time is a quick 'hi and bye, thanks for being alive' prayer), all they've done is squint their eyes in God's mirror. Do you know someone who refuses to open up his or her spiritual eyes any more than a squint?

------------ ◈ ------------

LESSON #2 DON'T FALL ASLEEP ON THE JOB!

The disciples had an important job to do. *So do you.* They were set as watchmen on the wall even while in the garden. Remember, Jesus is praying in the innermost parts of Gethsemane, and the disciples are supposed to be watching on the outermost parts. Their role is very important here. These men are like security guards at the airport. The only difference is, instead of protecting you from terrorism, they are busy dreaming of a white Christmas. Every time the disciples slept, not only did they suffer, but our Savior's safety was compromised. So, by asking them to stay awake, Jesus was saying on the one hand, "Stay awake and have my back." But on the other, He was teaching them a lesson about prayer and her enemy. You see, Jesus knew that prayer had an adversary. The disciples didn't. And if you didn't know that prayer has an adversary, now you know, too. This enemy is not skepticism or silence; it is sleepiness.

Think about it. Have you ever noticed how sleepy you become the moment you bend down to pray? The yawning happens almost immediately, and in those first five minutes, something within you is tugging you to give God a quick kiss on the cheek and go on about your day. You start telling yourself things like, "Get up and do something more productive." Or, even worse, you convince yourself out of prayer by saying, "I've got a long day ahead of me. I should just go back to sleep. Besides, my entire day will be thrown off if I don't get five more minutes." Meanwhile Jesus is saying to us, "My child, please don't fall asleep. If you do, the enemy will come in and wreak havoc in your house, ruin your family, and steal your stuff. Your role in the kingdom is too important." This is lesson #2.

------------ ◆ ------------

Lord, open up my eyes. Enter my mind and arrest my imagination.
Flood my words, my thoughts, and my memory with the endless rain of revelation.
Watch over me in prayer as I dive headfirst into Your presence. I'm awake now
and I don't ever want to fall asleep on my assignment again.

------------ ◆ ------------

THE LESSONS WE IGNORE TODAY BECOME TOMORROW'S LEFTOVERS

Now that we know the two lessons for the disciples, here are the questions for us to consider: How many tutoring sessions have we ignored (just like the disciples did), which eventually led to God making characters out of us? How many times has someone caught us sleeping on the job but instead of changing our patterns, we totally ignore the warning and do what we want to do anyway? Instead of watching out for signs and praying for understanding, we mute the Tutor's voice and fail the test. If you've ever done this before, join the club! This is what happened to me a few days ago. Welcome, readers, to part B of this self-exposure chronicle:

Time: Too early for roosters. Location: Jacksonville, Florida. I'm driving down an unfamiliar road in an unfamiliar car. It's pitch black dark. My flight is set to leave in 25 minutes. We're fifteen minutes away. My grandfather's Cadillac is cruising past everyone on the road. *Not bad for a 2003.* I crank up to 82 mph and start looking in every direction for cops or flashing lights. I need to get there. I cannot miss this flight because then I'll miss the connecting flight. Then it happened. Yup, IT. I felt the wheel shake a bit, and within seconds, the alignment on the car felt "off." I leaned over to the passenger side and whispered to my grandfather, "I think you need to get the wheel alignment checked out." He replied, "Yeah. I feel a pull on the right side of the—BOOM! *BOOM!* BOOMMM!!!!%*#!" And with those scary noises came a reality that I did not want to confront: the right tire had blown out without warning. The noise was horrifying, but even worse, I was driving the car! *I panicked.* I looked straight ahead and instinctively motioned my foot toward the brake pedal. Suddenly, I heard my grandfather scream, "DON'T HIT THE BRAKES!" The scream was louder than the boom, but God's voice rang higher than my grandfather's warning. I listened to his instructions and let the car slow itself down. Had I not been tutored through that unexpected event, I would've surely crashed that beautiful Cadillac into the median of a newly paved highway.

His words calmed me. His presence assured me. The car slowed down little by little. He whispered, "Now put your hazards on." I obeyed. Then he said, "Slowly ease your way over to the shoulder lane." I obeyed again. Within minutes, my brother and I were out of the car on this dark highway; one grandparent holding the flashlight, the other grandparent screaming "Jesus! Fix it! In the name of Jesus!" (of course that was my grandmother). And before I knew it, we were back on the road again. We changed the tire, replaced it with a spare, and arrived at the airport in enough time to safely board the plane.

SEEING GOD IN EVERYONE IN THE CAR

I hadn't known it at the time, but that was my Matthew 13 experience. It was God's parable to me, warning me about something that I didn't (and couldn't) anticipate. But like the disciples in Matthew 13, I didn't get it. I knew that my grandfather typified God's reliability in the midst of turmoil, and my grandmother's prayers reminded me that God is a very present help in the time of trouble. My brother's helpfulness even symbolized God's faithfulness during a crisis. But still, with all of the evidence in front me, I panicked. So God had no other choice but to turn my Matthew 13 into a Matthew 26.

My Matthew 26 happened on Saturday night, not even 24 hours after my Matthew 13. I was talking to friends about God's providence, and I got excited when I said, "We don't need man to validate our relationship or credentials in God!" *It's so much easier to tell others that.* I was going on and on about how God will reposition us if He finds us "Sleeping on the job," or, when He sees us working in a position that doesn't fulfill us spiritually. And not even five minutes later, I received an email of termination from my summer internship. *BOOM!#!* The words I read felt like the tire exploding on that dark highway toward Jacksonville Airport: "This is to communicate to you that the

Board has decided to dispense with your services as of today, July 11, 2009." My heart rate increased. I saw red. The sleeping worker at Seton Hall came to my mind, but then I realized....this wasn't my fault! I hadn't been sleeping on the job; I was serving. I mean, I didn't enjoy the experience one bit, but there was no reason for them to fire me! The sweat began pouring down my face. This had to be a major misunderstanding! I had to be dreaming! I heard God's voice whisper, "The battle is not yours" (2 Chronicles 20:15)[6] and "Vengeance is mine" (Romans 12:19)[7] and "Think it not strange" (1 Peter 4:12).[8] I heard all of these Scriptures—I really did, but before I knew it, I did the unthinkable— I hit the brakes. And I hit them hard! I slammed on those brakes and crashed (mentally, emotionally, spiritually) headfirst into the median. Despite the many practice exams, hidden messages and Scripture hints, I failed my test.

------------◈------------

Prayer: To the One who studies me even though You know my end from the beginning,

I recognize now that I have made quick decisions at times. I have acted out of anger and frustration. I rarely seek after Your wisdom and instruction first. Instead, I limp toward you after I crash my vehicle or receive a termination notice.

Please forgive me.

------------◈------------

HE GAVE ME A PARABLE, THEN HE MADE ME A PARABLE

1 Peter 4:12 Beloved, think it not strange ...

My email response did not feel Christian at all. I was typing so fast on my little blackberry, I thought for sure a key would soon pop off. I was furious. I slammed on those brakes and gave them a piece of my mind. *How dare they fire me? ME! Shaun Vermont Hamilton-Saunders!* (You know I was mad at that point!!) My ego was scarred. *I aint never been fired a day in my life.* My pride was bruised. *And by email? How professional is that?*

After about thirty solid minutes of rambling and overheating, I finally exited off of Anger Highway and realized what was happening. Just the day before, I was warned not to hit the brakes. Just a few years ago, I was reminded of the lady caught sleeping on the job. That memory was random, I thought, but God was using these real-life events to teach me a lesson. He was preparing me for that email, but I just couldn't put two and two together. I know I heard the Holy Spirit whisper those simple words to me: "Think it not strange…" and I didn't realize it then, but "Think it not strange" sounded so much like "Don't hit the brakes." "Think it not strange" rung in my ears like an annoying commercial tune as I wept in my car--*you know how after we're really angry and we've spoken our minds, we break down when no one sees us and we're left feeling vulnerable, empty and wrong*? Yup, that was me. Paining, hurting, heart throbbing. But, God comforted me. He gave me a parable, then He made me a parable, and when I still didn't understand, He spoke in the familiar: His Word.

If you listen when God speaks, one Word will save your life.

TAKE THE ALTERNATE ROUTE: WAKE UP AND DON'T HIT THE BRAKES

There is an alternate route, my friend. When you can't understand why things are going wrong in your life, wake up and pray. Watch your prayers and see God in the hidden messages around you. Try not to do like I did. Don't do like the disciples did. Don't hit the brakes. Instead, let God enter heavenly directions into your spiritual navigation system. When the unexpected happens, you don't need to panic. Just heighten your spiritual sensitivity by praying and listen out for God's whispering consolation. Allow the Scriptures to slow down your unstable automobile. I know this is easier said than done, but allow the testimonies of others to influence your life-decisions in a positive way. Pray for clarity, don't respond in anger. Be silent, don't speak before the proper time. *Breathe*, don't bottle up your thoughts and emotions. Pay attention. Hitting the brakes right now will only make matters worse. Leaving the church won't resolve anything. Talking about the pastor won't get you anywhere. Leaving your child in prison won't change the fact that he's there. Wake up and don't hit the brakes. Getting a divorce won't fix the battle going on in your mind. Don't hit the brakes. If anything, just take a break. Get out of the car and let God change the tire. Don't total your vehicle trying to prove to everyone else that you know how to drive. *Girl, you don't know what you doin'! Just be honest.* Turn your life license over to Jesus and let His identity, wisdom, smile, and experience become your own.

----------- ◈ -----------

God of all resources, help me to trust Your guidance. Speak to me in times of distress and confusion. Teach me to watch and pray. Teach me to watch while praying. Teach me to watch unto prayer; to pay attention and to listen. Through Christ, the True Co-Pilot and Tutor, Amen.

----------- ◈ -----------

Questions for Introspection
ଔ_____ ଥ

1) Who or what in your life has caused you to slam on the brakes? What irks you most about that person, place, or thing? Name it and then begin to pray for the subject in mind.

2) Recall a moment when God instructed you to "Wake up!" Did you obey? Did you fall back asleep after you realized no one was looking?

3) Has something transpired earlier this week that God could be using to communicate His will for your life? If so, write it down and wait for God to reveal its divine purpose.

Practical Points

1 Pray for the next person you see on the side of the road. If you are prompted by the Spirit to pull over, do so and assist in any way you can. You might not have the tools to offer them, but you do have access to God through prayer. Remember, God can and will protect, cover, and fix all things. Just trust Him.

2 All of us need physical rest so that our bodies can recharge. That's normal. But, if your "catnap" lasts for days at a time, you are no longer sleeping; you have fallen into a spiritual coma. Be alert so that rest does not turn into permanent recess. Don't allow your love for God and the zeal for God's mission to fall into remission. The harvest is too plentiful and the laborers are too few (Luke 10:2)[4] for us to take extended lunch breaks.

3 Make a decision today. Say it aloud if you have to: "I will not hit the brakes. The cares of this world will not swallow up my faith." God has been too good to allow a temporary inconvenience to cancel out His consistent providence.

4 Unexpected storms prove to me that I'm a sailor in God's boat, headed toward a destination to which the enemy doesn't want me to arrive. Think it not strange when these things happen. Suffering is a part of the resume, too.

5 Tell yourself to rejoice when you receive unexpected news. It's not the easiest thing to do immediately, but the more you tell yourself to rejoice, the easier your spirit begins to catch hold of it. Accept whatever God's will has allowed, and just watch; in a few minutes, you'll begin to see a shift in your emotions, in your spirit, and in your automobile. Don't hit the brakes!

Scripture Glossary

[1]**Matthew 13:24-25** *Another parable put he forth unto them, saying, The kingdom of heaven is likened unto a man which sowed good seed in his field: But while men slept, his enemy came and sowed tares among the wheat, and went his way.*

[2]**Matthew 26:36** *Then cometh Jesus with them unto a place called Gethsemane, and saith unto the disciples, Sit ye here, while I go and pray yonder.*

[3]**Matthew 26:40** *And he cometh unto the disciples, and findeth them asleep, and saith unto Peter, What could ye not watch with me one hour?*

[4]**Matthew 4:2** *And when he had fasted forty days and forty nights, he was afterward an hungered.*

[5]**Matthew 26:41** *Watch and pray that ye enter not into temptation: the spirit indeed is willing, but the flesh is weak.*

[6]**2 Chronicles 20:15** *And he said, Hearken ye, all Judah, and ye inhabitants of Jerusalem, and thou king Jehoshaphat, Thus saith the LORD unto you, Be not afraid nor dismayed by reason of this great multitude; for the battle is not yours, but God's.*

[7]**Romans 12:19** *Dearly beloved, avenge not yourselves, but rather give place unto wrath: for it is written, Vengeance is mine; I will repay, saith the Lord.*

[8]**1 Peter 4:12** *Beloved, think it not strange concerning the fiery trial which is to try you, as though some strange thing happened unto you.*

IRONING A SHIRT

My ½ Ironed Relation-shirt

CR_____EO

> *That he might present it to himself a glorious church, **not having spot, or wrinkle**, or any such thing; but that it should be holy and without blemish.*
> **Ephesians 5:27**

> *That he might sanctify and cleanse it with the washing of water by the word,*
> **Ephesians 5:26**

*G*etting dressed for the day can be overwhelming. I stood in my room one morning trying to put together a nicely coordinated outfit. I selected a tan button-down shirt, khakis, and some kicks to match my beige sweater vest. "This is what I want to look like," I thought to myself. Scrambling through my drawer to find a pair of matching socks, I suddenly realized I only had one pair left. *Bummer.* They were green, gray, and yellow socks and definitely were not going to work with the outfit. I had to make a decision. A very important decision. It felt like a life or death situation at the time. Don't laugh…*you're laughing,* but I'm serious. Here were the two options: do I put on yesterday's dirty socks (that no one would see anyway), or do I wear a pair of socks that did not coordinate with my outfit? The pressure was on, the clock was ticking, and Vanna White was nowhere in sight. I needed to decide. I needed to get to class!

After much prayer and fasting—a full three minutes of prayer and fasting—I put on the socks that did not match and thought nothing more of it. I quickly turned to iron the tan shirt that I had planned to wear underneath my beige sweater, but I had no time to iron it entirely because I was late. It didn't trouble me though. I had a plan and I was going to stick to it! The way *I* had planned it, I would use the sweater to cover up the wrinkles I did not iron. Easy, breezy, beautiful...cover up. *You know you've done it before! Quit trying to act like all of your outfits belong on a starch commercial.* That was my plan and nothing would change it. So, I strategically ironed all of the obvious places—the collar, the sleeves, and the areas below the bottom button—but I left the rest of the shirt more wrinkled than a crumpled up piece of paper in a recycling bin. *No one would know but me,* so I thought.

At that moment, a subtle voice whispered, "Rushing the ironing process, eh?"

I knew it was God trying to expose me again but I didn't have time to listen. I was not in the writing mood and I surely wasn't about to change my outfit. *Nope. Not now. Keep it moving, Shaun. You're going to be late for class. God will understand.* I got completely dressed and slid into my shoes feeling confident. I just knew Shaun would turn heads today. Turn heads alright. As I approached the door to leave, I took one final peak in the mirror and gasped in astonishment. *What...is...THAT....doing...there?* There was a big red spot smack dab in the middle of the sweater. The same sweater I depended on to cover up the wrinkles that I didn't have time to iron out. My breathing pattern increased. The room began to spin. Well, not really. But I did start to panic. The closer I got to the mirror, the more I realized I couldn't clean this one myself. The spot was too huge, too dark, and too permanent. I would have to take it to the cleaners, but you know I didn't have time to do that! So, I had to change my entire outfit. *Great. Just Great.* And guess what? As soon as I took off that spotted sweater, the wrinkles I tried to hide were staring back at me.

"Covering up only compresses issues that you're eventually going to have to deal with," whispered God.

Come on, Lord. Please, not today! I don't have time to go here with You. I huffed and I puffed and then I blew my sweater down into the hamper. I rushed over to the closet to change. I didn't want to change. I *had* to change. I had a reputation to uphold and an image to maintain. What would people think if I walked out of the house wearing a spotted shirt? "Not I," said the cat. People were not going to form a negative opinion about me if I could help it.

At this point, I'm sweating and frustrated. Not to mention, I'm really late for class by now. Things were not going the way I had planned! *How could I allow this to happen?* In a rush, I picked a sweater without thinking about coordination or anything. It no longer mattered how I looked. I just needed some clothes on. Thanks be to God, the sweater was perfectly pressed—*don't you just love those pullovers that never need to be ironed?* —so I slid it over my head and ran to the closet again to change my shoes. After all, the sweater was green, gray and yellow and I needed a... *Green. Gray. Yellow. Hmmm. That's funny.* I looked down at my feet and all of a sudden, the revelation hit me like a ton of bricks. Had someone installed a hidden camera in my room, you would've thought I was the craziest man alive.

"But I am watching. That's what I—"

OK! OK! Enough, God! Enough! We'll talk about this later! I slid my green, gray, and yellow socks into my shoes to match my green, gray, and yellow sweater (which I never planned to wear) and walked out of my room. The Lord began to speak to me again. I'm recapping, of course, but I vividly remember God saying something like:

"Trust Me to dress you. Trust Me to cleanse you. In My dressing room, you don't have to worry about wrinkles and spots. I sent my Son to die so that the outfit you call life would perfectly match My custom-made will for you. Just trust Me. I have the skills to coordinate things in your life that you could never take the credit for. Trust Me to dress you. Trust Me to cleanse you. Just trust Me."

These sentences sounded like heavenly music to my sweaty ears. So instead of whisking this moment away, I started writing this chronicle out in my palm pilot. Here is what I wrote....

I wonder how many Christians are guilty of wearing a half-ironed relationshirt. I wonder how many Christians claim to present themselves as living sacrifices, but in reality, very little of their living has been sacrificed for God's sake. Very little of the old nature has died because the new life is graffitied with the stains of yesteryear. I just wonder. I wonder how many of us wear a half-ironed shirt and don't even care about the impression our wrinkles might leave on someone who doesn't know God?

People can be tithe-givin' and bible-livin' saints and, at the same time, be guilty of a half-ironed relationship. We come to church every Sunday and model in Christian window displays, but depend on other humans to validate our freeze pose. Some of us show up early so that everyone will hear us praying. Others show up late so that people will notice our expensive outfit. We say a lot of big words while preaching to flaunt our intellect, but we render halfhearted prayers that seldom reach heaven. We sing fancily so that people can compliment our vocal range, but forget that church is about God, not us. Granted, intellect is impressive, musical talents are noteworthy, and compliments are fine, but what should matter most is that we come to church so that God can receive true worship.

The half-ironed relationshirt is not just a problem for individuals alone. A lot of churches obsess over the need to impress people as well. No matter the denomination, churches get caught in the bed of compromise all the time. Why? Because lots of preachers are preaching for the applause of man and not for the ovation of God (Galatians 1:10).[1] You'd be surprised to find out how many preachers think, "What do the people want to hear," before asking, "Lord, what do you want me to say? Many of us are so wrinkled up and spotted all over, but we don't even know it.

When are we going to learn how to trust God to dress us? I believe God is whispering these words to us for a reason, but we can't hear Him because we are too busy snatching the iron out of God's hand. We end up burning our blouses or tarnishing our trousers *not* because God wanted to punish us, but because we wanted to be in control. Or, because we wanted to cover up our secrets (as if God couldn't see them anyway). We need to learn to trust God with all of us! If we don't trust God, we'll trick ourselves and lie to others.

I tried it for years—I'll admit it—and it never worked. I tried to trick people into thinking that I was floating in the anointed bliss of God, but deep down, I had more wrinkles than Santa Clause's great-grandmother. *Now that's a lot of wrinkles.* I was lying to them and to myself. The spots got darker and the wrinkles became more obvious. But I kept on pulling down my shirt and covering my hand over the spot like nothing was wrong. Oh, trust me. I thought I knew how to cover up my spots and wrinkles, and so, I tried to; until I realized I was more invested in the cover-up than the clean-up. I would sit in service and not move at all, hoping that people would overlook me. I would sing, "I Surrender All" on Sunday, but pester God on Monday with questions like, *What am I doing here? This seems like a waste of time. Why am I wearing this particular job for so long? This doesn't match who I want to be in the future.* And on numerous occasions, I told God, "Lord, this goes in the opposite direction of what I want to do," as if He were the student and I was the teacher. But, this time, God used a wrinkled shirt and a spotted sweater to interrupt my ramblings, and then He sealed the incident with five simple words: "Trust Me to dress you." *To be continued...*

Eventually, I made it to class, but I couldn't pay attention to the lecture at all. Those words haunted me like the boogieman under a four-year old's bed. Revelation started to invade my mind like an unexpected guest. No matter what I did, I couldn't get that big red spot out of my head. *Fine, Lord. I'll give in. To the bat cave we go.* I cancelled everything else I had to do for the day, returned to my room, and opened my Bible. The Lord led me to the book of Ephesians.

CHANGE CLOTHES A.S.A.P.

Ephesians 6:11 Put on the whole armour of God, that ye may be able to stand against the wiles of the devil.

Ephesians 4:22-24 That ye put off concerning the former

conversation the old man, which is corrupt according to the deceitful lusts; and be renewed in the spirit of your mind; and that ye put on the new man, which after God is created in righteousness and true holiness.

Before I could trust God to dress me, I had to change clothes, take off my will, and willingly pursue God's dress code (spiritually speaking). In other words, I had to put on the whole armor and not just the articles I liked best. You know how we do. Everyone likes the helmet of salvation, but who wants to wear a breastplate called righteousness? A breastplate is heavy and ugly. *Yuck! No thanks, God. I think the shield is large enough to cover me. And wait a minute. Doesn't righteousness mean I have to give up doing wrong so I can walk right? No thanks. Oh. And by the way, Lord. I'm not putting on the belt of truth. Not only is it a bit girly, but truth isn't the 'in' thing to wear as a Christian anymore. In fact, when someone asks, "How are you?" I don't even bother to tell the truth. Why tell how I really feel? No one really wants to hear it nor do I want to tell it. Not to mention, the last person I told the truth to exposed my wounds and hurt me. So, no thanks. I'll pass the iron over that part too. And while I'm at it, I'll skip the section that says "preparation of the gospel of peace" for my feet. Who wants to prepare anymore? I don't have time to prepare! My CD needs to be in stores next week! My book must be published tomorrow! The gospel of peace? No, thanks. I'll walk barefoot.*

A lot of Christians think this way, but no one knows it because, as I said earlier, when Sunday morning comes, we are picture perfect and dressed for the occasion. This was my biggest problem. I was more concerned about being picture perfect than I was God dependent. I didn't want to "change clothes." I *had* to. I had come to place so much trust in others' perception of me (and my spiritual appearance) that I had stopped leaning and depending on God. My Christian walk was no longer focused on God's will. I could care less about trusting in the Lord with all of my heart. There were too many people to impress. Too many concerts and conferences to attend. I had a reputation to maintain. The Christian thing had become about pleasing me(n). And not before long, I was measuring my sacred relationship by the ruler of human perception. I was using someone else's badly tuned piano to play my life song to the Lord. God was no longer my Source. He was simply a jumper cable. He was my AAA service, and I called Him only if my car needed a jumpstart. I ran to Him after people let me down. I spoke to Him if and only if things did not turn out my way. I was not a worshipper. I was a wobbler. *Can you relate?* If I'm on your street, just say, "Ouch!"

Prayer: Father, I have a confession to make.

I'm guilty of allowing the swiftness of my days to spot up my garment and prevent me from seeking You first.

Please forgive me.

At the same time, please don't think I've fully arrived. I'm growing out of this tendency. If the *whole* truth were exposed, I would tell you that I still find myself wobbling from time to time. I still find myself overly concerned about what others think of me. I still catch myself looking around at others before looking up to God. But, this chronicle serves as a reminder from God to me, and every time I read it, God ministers to my approval addiction. So, you be encouraged. I know it hurts to see God in your wrinkles, but reader, if your faith is placed in people and not in God, you've got to change clothes as soon as possible. Paul encourages us to put our faith in the power of God, and not in the wisdom of men (1 Corinthians 2:5).[2] Jeremiah curses the man that trusts in another man (Jeremiah 17:5).[3] David vowed to place His trust in God and God alone (Psalm 71:1).[4] *If our hearts tell us where our treasures are* (Luke 12:34),[5] *then I believe our trust reveals to us where our faith is.* Please understand. You will see heavy consequences if your faith in men supersedes your faith in God.

But let me be clear here. These Scriptures don't necessarily mean we can never confide in one another. We can and we should. However, when we confess our faults to one another (James 5:16),[6] we must always remember three key disclaimers about the trust factor. First, it is *always* better to trust God than to put confidence in man (Psalm 118:8).[7] Why? Because unfaithful is not in God's dictionary. All God knows is fidelity. All God knows is loyalty, and all God knows is truthfulness, so you can trust God with all of yourself. He will never ever let you down! Furthermore, if you invest trust into someone who does not know God, then your investment is, at best, a risky gamble, and at worst, destined for bankruptcy. I've got to tell it to you straight. Proverbs warns us by saying, "Confidence in an unfaithful man...is like a broken tooth and a foot out of joint" (Proverbs 25:19).[8] So, if you're wondering why things are irreparably broken in your life, maybe you've invested too much trust into broken stock, broken teeth, and broken bones. You're asking your pre-saved beautician for advice and she has no clue who Christ is. You're checking the horoscope to guide you, and the people who write those things aren't thinking about God's divine purpose for your life. Broken information breeds broken revelation. It's almost like receiving advice from a bank teller about cardiology. The two just don't match up. Very few bank tellers I know have a medical degree hanging on their office wall! Please take inventory now. Who knows most of your business? Are they hooked into the Source? Have you told them more than you've confessed to God? If the persons you trust do not believe in the same God you believe in, tell me where lies the evidence of their faith? How can you expect that man to keep his word to you if he doesn't know the Word for himself? He can't keep his word any more than a broken tooth can maintain its original shape.

Don't be a spiritless mannequin, standing poised, looking perfect but powerless. Many Christians are so "perfect" that they have become unusable, and those who need God are not impressed by our alleged perfection. Remove the sweater of perfection, expose your wrinkles and let God iron them out so you can become God's living sacrifice.

Now, here's the last nugget about the trust factor. God's

perfection is the only characteristic that gives credence to *Christ-ians*. Please don't place heavy trust weight on another Believer. Even the Believer is flawed with the Flawless One within her. Believers break promises too, boo! The Scripture says with God all things are possible, absolutely! But with mankind, all things are capable of failure (Romans 3:23).[9] Get this, get this, get this. If ever you hear me saying, "I trust you" to someone, what I really mean is, "I trust the God in you." Now, you just make sure that God is in you! Why do I say that? Well, partly because I've discovered that even with God, human beings can mess up. Hey, I still mess up! I've let myself down too many times to function as a reliable source. Which is why Proverbs 3:5 encourages us to trust God and lean not to our own understanding. In other words, trusting yourself can't beat trusting God (much less trusting anyone else). Just learn to trust God. That way, we won't be let down when (not if) people fail us.

RUSHING THE IRONING PROCESS

I had to trust God. Definitely. Then, I had to stop rushing God. *Pause.* I want to talk about rushing for a moment. I suspect most of us are in the condition we're in today because we rushed over a season that God intended to use as preparation for this season. And now we're wobbling and limping, and covering our spots all because we moved too quickly, but we're too prideful to admit it. Just examine yourself as I examine myself. Have you, my dear friend, ever rushed God's ironing process? Was your last year anything like my hurried morning? *I know. I know.* You figured people weren't going to see the part of you that was most

-------------◈-------------
Prayer: Lord, like a wrinkly shirt needs ironing, so too do we need to be pressed by your Holy steamer daily.
We don't want to hang on the pews like an unworn blouse or an outdated suit.
Wear us for your glory.
-------------◈-------------

wrinkled anyway, so you excused the process away by saying things like, "I'm human. God understands…" or, "The grace of God will cover me." And yes, I am grateful for the grace of God. I truly am. But, I cannot applaud the excuses of man. Listen, friends. We've got to take responsibility for our actions. "God will understand" does not mean God will approve. There are a lot of things we do that God does not approve of, but God doesn't impose on our daily routine. He didn't make us robots. Oh sure, God sees us doing things that disappoint Him and misguide us, but God doesn't interrupt our phone call even when we're wasting time talking to people who mean us no good. He created us as human beings with choose-ability (Deuteronomy 30:19b).[10] God knows we are students, but He gives us a schedule to see if we will choose Him over our extra-curricular activities sometimes. God knows we are parents, working two jobs, but He gives us personal days to see if we'll ever spend time with Him. Just examine yourself. Are all of your days-off simply days-on for other errands and worldly affairs? When is the last time you set the alarm to wake up for prayer and didn't hit the snooze button? God knows we have responsibilities to our elderly relatives, but that does not change the fact that God desires intimate moments with each of us. It does not change the fact that even on our busiest day, we still find time to waste time. It does not alter the fact that God sees us make time for sin but avoid time with Him. Yes, God understands. In fact, God's grace is evidence of His understanding heart. But, we shouldn't use the grace of God as a "get out of prayer and meditation free" card.

After all of our excuses, what God really understands is that we don't love Him like we say we do; and God is hurt by this reality. But here's the good news: God is willing to overlook your rushing tendency and establish a true relationship with you *if you are willing to submit to the ironing process.* Are you?

SUBMIT? I DON'T KNOW ABOUT ALL OF THAT.

Ephesians 5 is about submission. It is traditionally used to speak of the love between a husband and wife, but Ephesians 5 is not centrally about marriage roles and responsibilities. It's centrally about submission to God. That means, a husband shouldn't turn to these verses as scriptural backing for putting his wife in her place. No! No! No! We've got it all wrong. If you read the chapter carefully, you'll understand why Paul doesn't write, "This epistle must be understood as the perfect Christian model for husbands and wives." Instead, Paul explains at the conclusion of the letter, "...I speak concerning Christ and the church" (Ephesians 5:32).[11] You see, Paul is up to something here. He is trying to articulate the mystery of God's love in relatable terms and he uses the husband/wife imagery to communicate in comprehensible lingo how Christ loved the church so much that He was willing to "give himself for us as an offering and sacrifice to God" (Ephesians 5:2).[12] But even Paul's analogy doesn't do it justice.

Many Christians love to boast, "I'm married to Christ," and many will wear the righteousness of God nametag on Sunday, but few of us submit to the ironing process of daily sanctification. Even fewer of us live as if our love for God exceeded our love for our spouse or family member(s). Saints, let's get our priorities right!

Which brings me to a sidebar point. *Justice.* We really need to give better justice to the Scriptures. How we read Scripture says a lot about who matters most (us or God; our way or God's way). Readers, when you study Scripture, learn how to consume all of it and not just the appetizing parts you like. If you skip the entrée in Ephesians 5 and head straight for the dessert cart, you'll starve your spirit and suffer from indigestion. Please don't misinterpret these key verses. Before the husband and wife component in verse 21-25, Paul admonishes the church to, "[submit] yourselves to one another." He uses this representation to emphasize how important it is to submit to God. How do I know? Well, after the analogy, Paul returns again to the unique role Christ plays in purifying His church. This is oh so very clear to me. Ephesians 5 is all about God and the art of submission.

But what is submission? *So glad you asked.* Submission, to me, means to get underneath something and obey its mission. We submit to God by positioning ourselves like a helpless shirt on God's holy ironing board. We just lay there and let God do what God does best—iron us until we are wrinkle-free. Now, here's another disclaimer: sometimes God has to iron us longer than we want to be ironed. And most times, God is a really slow ironer! I have personally been under the heat of tribulation for weeks at a time, and still, God wouldn't let up! One thing after another: first the marriage, then an unexpected bill, then the doctor's report, then there are issues between the church and the landowner. You know how it is. God presses us, creases us, and then holds us up in the mirror and, of course, He finds another wrinkle. *Nope. Shaun's attitude is still not right.* He irons some more. *Nope. His motive for ministry is self-absorbed.* He irons some more. *Did I just hear him curse?* STEAM! STEAM! STEAM! He irons some more. No matter how holy I think I am, God will always reveal another area upon which I can improve.

Submission is a necessary part of the process even though nobody wants to go through it. In fact, all of us I bet would opt for a shortcut. We would rather demand God to give us the portion to which we are entitled and avoid the pain that comes along with the ironing process. But let me remind you—you are not God. Neither am I. And, once we stop trying to control things and simply submit to God's will for our lives, then God can iron His thoughts on our mind, cleanse our

-----------◈-----------

God's iron will always press the bad out so that your good side can show. The process is working for your good even though it's hot sometimes and uncomfortable almost all of the time.

-----------◈-----------

body, and renew our spirit. This process isn't punishment. God just wants to see you at your best. So, save yourself some starch and steam, and just submit to the press and say, "Yes!" to the process.

TO BE SANCTIFIED IS TO BE PUT ON RESERVE

Submission is only half of the process, however. The second variable is sanctification. What does it mean to be sanctified—without all the deep churchy words? *So glad you asked.*

Well, to me, to be sanctified is to be put on reserve for a special occasion. It's like the wedding cake that the bride-to-be requests for her reception. After she picks that cake, no one can touch it. The cake is reserved for her use and for her wedding. This is a parable for sanctification. Or, sanctification is like that beautiful white shirt that you remove from the washing machine and hang outside for a few hours to dry. After the shirt dries, you hang it up in your closet to be worn at a particular time, for a particular purpose. In a like manner, God sanctifies us so that He can wear us in the earth. This whole process is really not for ourselves, but in order that God might wear us as it pleases Him (1 Corinthians 12:18).[13] When we submit to the process, other spotted garments, through our sanctification, can be brought to the Cleaners. The cake is served to those who will attend the party and the garment is cleaned so that others might see the benefits of a good wash, rinse, and dry. We are not sanctified to just sit idly

------------ ◈ ------------

To the All Knowing God, So you want truth? Here's the truth. Most times, when I look in the mirror, I really don't like what I see. But before I knew what a reflection was, you loved me. Even after I tried to cover up the shadows of insecurity and spots of sin, you removed my shame and loved me as I was. Now Lord, please meet me where I am.

------------ ◈ ------------

on the church pew and fan ourselves. No! God wears some of us as pastors in the pulpit or preachers in the barbershop. And God wear some of us in the street as an evangelist or in the classroom as a teacher. He sanctifies us to preach the gospel wherever there is a listening congregation. So, there is a purpose behind sanctification. God never sanctifies without commissioning you, at some point, to an unsanctified place.

MIRROR MIRROR ON THE WALL, IS GOD REALLY LOOKING AFTER ALL?

Proverbs 15:3 The eyes of the LORD are in every place, beholding the evil and the good.

The answer is yes. God is looking at us all the time. God scans every part of our outfit, even the parts we try to hide. God sees all. In fact, there is a spiritual surveillance camera peering over every move we make, every thought we think, and recording every word we say. Let me tell you a sidebar story that will emphasize the point.

My mom is a daycare director. One year, the state of NJ installed surveillance cameras in each classroom so teachers would know they were being watched. My mother rarely reviews the cameras, but one small recording device will change a caretaker forever. Someone they could not physically see was able to look in on their classroom at any time. Her teachers became more attentive, sang louder, and smiled more. They stopped text messaging on the clock and learned how to appropriately discipline children. What a difference knowing you're under surveillance makes! Which proves that some of us don't really believe God sees us. If we really believe that God sees us, we would be a little less talkative and a lot more prayerful. If we would realize the omnipresence of God in our lives, and take seriously the Scripture that says, "The eyes of the Lord are in every place, beholding the evil and the good," (Proverbs 15:3)[14] then we would live a holy and acceptable life everyday as opposed to putting on a show on Sunday. *Pause.* You do realize Sunday service has, for many churches, become a matinee where people replace their popcorn for Bibles and enjoy a nice little show, right? Bible Study, then, is the dress rehearsal for Sunday's production and as long as you keep the audience entertained, they will come back for more. *But wait! Not too much entertainment, preacher! I've got to take the girls to the mall and pregame is in an hour.* I'm on another tangent I know, but this is dishonorable in the sight of God and someone must speak out about it. People are hiding behind the production and weeping behind the "Amen." Christians are in real pain and stand in need of ministry. Who will respond to the insecure and ashamed after the fat lady sings? Perhaps the muslim or atheist will if the church doesn't do something quick.

I'm back. I promise. God sees us. That's the point. If we believed in God's omnipresence, we wouldn't order quick prayer nuggets at the drive-thru window of Bedside Church of the Louder Day Snores. We would feel convicted about demanding our blessing "To Go" all the time when we know that God is longing for a sit-down meal. We would make sure to have a nutritious and worshipful conversation with God before other things got in the way of our one-on-one time.

How important is God to you, and how important is the God in you (1 Corinthians 6:19)?[15] If God is as important as you profess, then move beyond the minimum wage, dollar menu quickies, and nurture the spirit of God within. Embrace all that God has for you and spend quality time with Him. Believe me when I say, those intimate hours you dedicate to God will make a major difference in the long run.

A MIRROR WILL REVEAL ALL BLIND SPOTS

John 17:17 Sanctify them through thy truth: thy word is truth.

In the mirror was where I realized the problem was me. I had allowed my own shirt to get wrinkled; not the devil, not a distraction. I did. The same way I would toss my clothes across the floor after a long workday, I had begun to throw my spirit-man (my heart, my investments, my time) all over the place. I allowed my mind to wander into areas clearly labeled NO TRESPASSING. Sometimes, I would even allow other people to sample my clothing without God's permission. You know how it goes. We let someone borrow our hearts for a season with the hopes that they will share theirs. And then, after we have completely given all of ourselves, they throw us away like a worthless rough draft. How could I expect my clothes (and by clothes I mean my spiritual garments) not to get wrinkled if I was constantly allowing other people to influence my actions and decisions? When I realized all of this, the scripture, "Sanctify them with thy truth" popped into my head (John 17:17).[16] You see, seeing the truth was all a part of the sanctification process, too. That means, dear reader, if you're ever going to be cleansed the right way, you've got to learn how to find freedom in the truth. Look in the mirror and deal with your naked reflection. The truth is ugly sometimes and it is painful, but it will free you (John 8:32).[17]

And those spots. They were my fault, too. No one else was responsible for the spotted sweater. I was. The spots were on *my* sweater. Remember, it wasn't until I put the sweater on and looked in the mirror that I even noticed the spot. I had been ironing, rushing, and focusing on my cover up so much that I missed the obvious stain looking right back at me. Can't you see God in this? Here we are focusing on how we will hide our wrinkly bad habits from everyone else, but when we look at our reflection, God shows us the bigger issue. The blind spots. Oh, yes. We've all got them and I don't think I'm alone in avoiding the blind spots. Blind spots are areas you can't see because you're so busy looking at someone else's. Blind spots are those beams in your eye even though you ridicule the mote in someone else's (Matthew 7:5).[18] Blind spots. The worst blind spot is not outside of your visual limitation; it is the one you see but you can't *see*.

When I looked in the mirror and paused to hear what God was saying to me, I suddenly realized the Lord was using this spotted sweater to tell me, "Shaun, the real spot is right up under your nose." In the same way, I suspect that the root of your issue is in front of you, but you can't see it because you're always overlooking the obvious clues. You know, like that man you're engaged to. He switches around the house right in front of you and he's always making comments about another man's attractiveness. The evidence is there. Don't ignore it. Or, your teenage daughter. She keeps saying things like, "So ma! If I had a baby like Shirley (another teenager)…" or, "Deacon So and So said he'll cook for me again after church…but he said for you to stay home. He'll bring me back at 11." Deacon So and So is 20 years older, three times divorced, and always avoiding you in church. Listen. Before you go on a 40-day fast, open your eyes and look around. Is it possible that something shady is going on? I'm not suggesting that we type cast anyone, but I am urging you to smell the "something ain't right" coffee before your daughter's virginity is poured into the cup of a pedophile. It is very likely that your precious little angel is sexually active or at least very curious. So, before she ends up pregnant, you've got to ask those hard questions that get to the root of the issue.

As painful as it is to admit, some of the greatest preachers have been violated by someone in church. We can't ignore the probabilities. That's all. Flesh is flesh and temptation knows no prejudice.

There's something underneath. The spot of idolatry, the blemish of pride, and the stain of hatred are the root problems. But when the flower buds, all you see is that little girl's promiscuous behavior or that handsome boy's conceited disposition. You've got to focus on the spots and not simply the wrinkles by themselves. An overeater or a murderer might answer the phone, but the digits that show up on the caller ID are Depression, Insecurity, Anger and Loneliness (D.I.A.L). Learn how to listen out for the D.I.A.L. tones. Voices will trick you but tones cannot. You've got to know who the strongman is in the house and pay more attention to him than you do his kiddy imps (Mark 3:27).[19] This is not speculation or a cute acronym. This is biblical:

Ephesians 5:5 for this ye know, that no whoremonger, nor unclean person, nor covetous man, **who is an idolator**, hath any inheritance in the kingdom of Christ.

Ephesians 5:5 points to the umbrella of idolatry. Idolatry is the root problem. But, whoredom, uncleanness, and covetousness stick their little heads out of the larger umbrella. So we never really *see* the black umbrella of idolatry because the colorful raincoats of whoredom, uncleanness, or covetousness are more striking to the eye. *Lord, help us to see the wrinkles as well as the spots!* Don't you see where the church has gone wrong? All this time, we've been half-ironing our issues away and we have accustomed ourselves to preaching over the addiction and around the hypocrisy, when God wants to uproot the seeds that have been planted beneath our devilish desires. If we only focus on covering up one sin, we forget about the sinful nature that is at work beneath every sin we knowingly (and unknowingly) commit against God. God is saying, in other words, "Your entire sin garden must die, not only the flowers of fornication." Hear ye the word of the Lord. If you don't allow God to kill the seed and plant righteousness in you, then two weeks later you'll need another clipping. Then two days later, another clipping. When will it stop lest you dig out the root?

There is something beneath the surface. Search out the bigger issue. Ask God to reveal to you what lies beneath your cycle of bad decisions. You may be beating yourself up because you're not getting A's on your report card, but the root of the issue is that you lack discipline. So, before you accuse your professor of racism, sit still for more than two hours and ban yourself from Facebook.com. You need discipline. You don't need demons cast out of you (or your teacher for that matter). You may think your pastor is jealous of your anointing because he won't let you preach. You sing better than him, so to you, he's hindering your gift. When in reality, you never come to church on time. You have a chronic problem with timeliness. Get to the root and dispense with the shallow stuff. If we're ever going to be purified, God will have to move us beyond the surface levels of excuse and blame in order to deliver us from the root of evil.

THE WATER THAT CLEANSES IS HIS WORD

But we're not done. Yes, our spots must be removed and our wrinkles must be ironed so that God's purpose can be fulfilled on earth, and most importantly, so that we are prepared for Christ's return (Ephesians 5:27).[20] I got that part. But, *how* are they removed? How do the wrinkles disappear? Are spots removed if I go to church and give a lot of money to homeless people? *No.* Are the wrinkles ironed out if I work everyday to rid my mind of all filthy thoughts? *No.* What detergent will Christ use if I'm really, really dirty? Clorox? *No! No! No!* These were the questions and frustrations that I brought to God as I sat down to learn. I certainly believed that Christ was coming back for a church without spot or wrinkle—I had heard the verse a million times in church—but I didn't know how it would be accomplished. I mean, to me, His coming back would be a waste of time. Jesus would return and find no one pure and everything spotted because we humans are a mess! Even the purist of us is not spotless. So, I really didn't understand how humans would ever become clean enough for God to accept us...until the Holy Spirit led me to verse 26. Read Ephesians 5:26-27 slowly:

Ephesians 5:26-27 That *he* might sanctify and cleanse *it* with the washing of water by the word, That *he* might present *it* to himself a glorious church, **not having spot**, **or wrinkle**, or any such thing; but that *it* should be holy and without blemish.

I really want you to understand this Scripture so I'm going to take my time. The *"He"* in these verses refers to Jesus. He is the one who will cleanse it. The "it" refers to the church. The church is the one who is spotted (not the "world," but the church...but that's for another day). Remember, Ephesians 5 is all about Christ and the church. He (Jesus) cleanses it (the church) so that we can experience the beauty of holy matrimony. Why does He cleanse it? Because He has to. He is not only committed to us, but He is submitted to us. He works under our mission and we work under His. When Jesus saw His bride in danger, He got under her mission and vowed to make things better. He wasn't about to let us walk down the aisle spotted. So, instead of sitting above the clouds and laughing at our speckled gown, He stepped into our universe, and became the Planner and the Purifier, the Presenter and the Preparer. He prepared the church by purifying her, and then He married the thing that was dirty before He touched it. While we were yet sinners, He died (Romans 5:8).[21] He knew the perfect cake to serve at our reception: Himself, and, He served us Himself so that we would one day be able to serve Him to others. You see, He works under our mission and we work under His.

But He didn't stop there. He purified us on earth so that our glory garment could match His glory tux in heaven. We had to coordinate with Christ for our "Welcome Home" reception. And He did this because He loves us. He did this so that you could once again recognize your own beauty and worth in Him. *You are beautiful. You are beautiful.* He did this because He values you. *You are valuable. You are valuable.* Don't forget that. I don't care how many wrinkles appear on your shirt and I'm not concerned about the generational dirt that has fallen on you because of family dysfunction. Christ values you, the church, as His bride. We are His gift and He is our glory, in spite of the fact that we did nothing to make that gift beautiful.

Always remember this: regardless of what we've done, Christ is still in covenant with creation. And a true covenant keeper is committed to his word even if his significant other defaults. Yes, we damaged our garments, but God kept His Word. Yes, we spotted ourselves and God could have retaliated, but instead, God reconciled us back to Himself (by His sacrificial death on a cross) so that His Word would remain pure and undefiled. He kept His Word and personally carried our sins to

Calvary's Cleaners. And with that same Word, Christ thee Wed. Christ has promised to return for us so that He can present us to Himself. Jesus keeps on keeping His Word, and that's why the only product we need to wash us is...His Word, you got it! Not our tithes or our white garments, but His Word. Not our good deeds or our prayer beads, but His Word. Do you get it? Do you see it now? Everything and everyone else will fail, but the Word will stand forever (Luke 21:33).[22] When I sat down on Him, His Word stood up for me. Others might see me as sinful, but God sees me as spotless. God sees us differently because He *is* the Cleaners. He's dipping you in water while others are making fun of your swimming trunks. He's saving your marriage while others are criticizing you for staying with your unfaithful husband. God sees us differently than others. The thoughts He thinks toward us are not only connected to our present, but also to our end (Jeremiah 29:11).[23] No man, woman, boy, or girl I know has ever loved me like this before! What a loving God we serve!

TRUST GOD TO DRESS YOU:
THE CONCLUSION OF THE WHOLE MATTER

I realize now that I had been asking the wrong questions. I assumed that I had something to do with my cleaning process. I didn't. I thought I was supposed to grab the iron at some point and iron my own wrinkles out. I wasn't. The only thing God asked me to do was trust Him. He wanted my surrender, not my second opinion. He wanted my "yes," not my "but, maybe." All I really had to do was give Him permission to wash me. *You should do the same.* Christ is polite. He won't come into your heart until you open the door and let Him in (Revelation 3:20).[24] He won't iron your shirt until you give it to Him. He won't take your life. You have to offer it up to Him. *Listen.* When I gave my life over to Christ, I signed a permission slip that said between the spaces of my signature, "Not my will but thy will be done." If you are saved, you did, too. If you are not saved (meaning you don't know Jesus personally and relationally), I recommend the gift of salvation to you. I don't want you to burn your beautiful blouse called life. I don't want you to look up and realize that life has passed you by. You might not be where you think you need to be, but truthfully, no one is. Have faith in God. Trust God. Stop trying to scrub off your spots and stains. You can't get this one out by yourself anyway. In fact, if you had the power to purify yourself, you wouldn't need a Savior and Christ wouldn't have had to die.

If you take nothing else from this chronicle, remember the words, "Trust Me to dress you." Let the One who made you, cleanse you. Allow Him into your closet so He can rearrange your life and change your way of thinking. God wants to set you apart for His glory. Covering up won't fix it. Adding layers to conceal your wrinkles won't make them disappear. Learn to trust God with every part of you. God is a whole lot older than us. He's got us by eternity.

And yes, it'll be uncomfortable when God presses us—I won't lie to you—but walk out of this dressing room with assurance. God exposes us in order to cleanse us, not to condemn us (Romans 8:1).[25] He knows what we hide up our sleeves and yet He loves us still. So go on...remove the sweater of perfection, expose your wrinkles, and let God iron them out so you can be made into a living sacrifice. God wants to clean you from the inside-out. If you let him, God will put your unmatched socks in divine coordination with His plans for your life.

------------ ◈ ------------

Sanctifier of all things impure, I know that Destiny is waiting for me to submit completely and trust You fully. Please help me to throw my wants into the dirty clothes hamper. Transform my half-ironed relation-shirt into a whole-hearted relationship. All I want is You. All I need is You. In Christ's name. Amen.

------------ ◈ ------------

Questions for Introspection

1) List three of your "wrinkles." Literally, write them on the side margins of this section. How long have you been trying to hide these areas in your life? Why?

2) Do other people know about your spots and wrinkles? How might confession to God and confession to neighbor help to relieve you?

Practical Points

1 God has a plan for each of us. It was God who stored our future into the memory card of eternity long before we were born. Because God knows, we don't need to know. Trust God to dress you and trust God to cleanse you. If you stay in the will of God, you will receive assurance and security. God is responsible for each and every member of His body. God will handle all of the details.

2 Before God's Spirit can indwell you, He must transform you from dark to light, old to new, sinner to saint (2 Corinthians 5:17).[26] There is something beneath the surface. Search out the bigger issue and stop trying to cover up the itsy bitsy problem. The lifelong goal for every Christian should be to cling onto Jesus everyday so we can stay submitted, sanctified, and pure (John 15:3).[27]

3 When God shows you how you look in His mirror, no matter how spotty or ugly, give God praise for it! Be grateful that He didn't let you walk out of your house another day without correcting you, reproving you, and changing you. He's a greater friend than some of the people you "trust." They'll let you go about your day and never tell you that there's food stuck in your teeth.

4 We are not sanctified and cleansed so that we can flaunt our white garments, boast in our Hebrew and Greek interpretations, or look down on those who don't know Christ. No. We are cleansed so that Christ can use us as models of His glory. We ought to wear His name wherever we go since our primary career is to carry the cross daily, follow Him, and handle the steam that comes with it. Go through the ironing process and watch God transform your entire outlook. Remember, if there is no steam, the crispness of the crease won't last.

5 The Word of God is a mirror that shows us our reflection from God's perspective. But remember, God sees us whether we look into the mirror of His Word or not. Whether we pray, whether we go to church, whether we get out of the bed, God sees us. God is sort of like the picture that won't stop staring at you even after you turn away. He looks upon us with that same haunting gaze. God won't take His eyes off of you because He loves you.

Scripture Glossary

[1]**Galatians 1:10** *For do I now persuade men, or God? or do I seek to please men? for if I yet pleased men, I should not be the servant of Christ.*

[2]**1 Corinthians 2:5** *That your faith should not stand in the wisdom of men, but in the power of God.*

3Jeremiah 17:5 *Thus saith the LORD; Cursed be the man that trusteth in man, and maketh flesh his arm, and whose heart departeth from the LORD.*

4Psalm 71:1 *In thee, O LORD, do I put my trust: let me never be put to confusion.*

5Luke 12:34 *For where your treasure is, there will your heart be also.*

6James 5:16 *Confess your faults one to another, and pray one for another, that ye may be healed. The effectual fervent prayer of a righteous man availeth much.*

7Psalm 118:8 *It is better to trust in the LORD than to put confidence in man.*

8Proverbs 25:19 *Confidence in an unfaithful man in time of trouble is like a broken tooth, and a foot out of joint.*

9Romans 3:23 *For all have sinned, and come short of the glory of God.*

10Deuteronomy 30:19b *...I have set before you life and death, blessing and cursing: therefore choose life, that both thou and thy seed may live.*

11Ephesians 5:32 *This is a great mystery: but I speak concerning Christ and the church.*

12Ephesians 5:2 *And walk in love, as Christ also hath loved us, and hath given himself for us an offering and a sacrifice to God for a sweetsmelling savour.*

131 Corinthians 12:18 *But now hath God set the members every one of them in the body, as it hath pleased him.*

14Proverbs 15:3 *The eyes of the LORD are in every place,* *beholding the evil and the good.*

[15]**1 Corinthians 6:19** *What? know ye not that your body is the temple of the Holy Ghost which is in you, which ye have of God, and ye are not your own?*

[16]**John 17:17** *Sanctify them through thy truth: thy word is truth.*

[17]**John 8:32** *And ye shall know the truth, and the truth shall make you free.*

[18]**Matthew 7:5** *Thou hypocrite, first cast out the beam out of thine own eye; and then shalt thou see clearly to cast out the mote out of thy brother's eye.*

[19]**Mark 3:27** *No man can enter into a strong man's house, and spoil his goods, except he will first bind the strong man; and then he will spoil his house.*

[20]**Ephesians 5:27** *That he might present it to himself a glorious church, not having spot, or wrinkle, or any such thing; but that it should be holy and without blemish.*

[21]**Romans 5:8** *But God commendeth his love toward us, in that, while we were yet sinners, Christ died for us.*

[22]**Luke 21:33** *Heaven and earth shall pass away: but my words shall not pass away.*

[23]**Jeremiah 29:11** *For I know the thoughts that I think toward you, saith the LORD, thoughts of peace, and not of evil, to give you an expected end.*

[24]**Revelation 3:20** *Behold, I stand at the door, and knock: if any man hear my voice, and open the door, I will come in to him, and will sup with him, and he with me.*

[25]**Romans 8:1** *There is therefore now no condemnation to them*

which are in Christ Jesus, who walk not after the flesh, but after the Spirit.

[26]**2 Corinthians 5:17** *Therefore if any man be in Christ, he is a new creature: old things are passed away; behold, all things are become new.*

[27]**John 15:3** *Now ye are clean through the word which I have spoken unto you.*

COMPLAINING ON THE TELEPHONE

Learning to be Content

ᘓ_____ᘒ

Not that I speak in respect of want: for I have learned in whatsoever state I am, therewith to be content.
Philippians 4:11

And when the people complained, it displeased the Lord: and the Lord heard it; and his anger was kindled; and the fire of the Lord burnt among them, and consumed them that were in the uttermost parts of the camp.
Numbers 11:1

I graduated from a middle-class suburban high school in New Jersey. Most of my classmates were of European descent, but regardless of their race, I had some great friends in high school. Truly I did. They were positive, they were smart, and they were very influential people. They said the word "like" (I've got a, like, soccer game and, like, I need to, like, go to the mall) one too many times during our conversations at lunch, but overall, they were great people to know. Most of my friends loved the Lord and they would never harm a soul even if someone deserved a good punch in the face. They were not perfect though and neither was I. Now that I've reached perfection, however, needless to say, I have had to cut those friends off to find some other, better friends. Just kidding! But anyway, my friends had something in common that I didn't really pay attention to until years later. They all had a tendency to complain about the smallest little matters. *Drum roll, please.* Ladies and Gentlemen, I introduce to some and present to others…the Complaining Crew.

So there was my one friend. We'll call her Sally. Sally was the kind of girl who had everything going for her and for some reason, she couldn't see it. Sally could've become a doctor. Sally could've become a lawyer. Sally could very well be running for both the President of the United States and the Ambassador of Jamaica right now. She was just that great, and yet, Sally always had something to complain about. Her face was too small, her waist was too big, her blood was too red, and her water was too....watery. Sally was a super complainer! She graduated as the salutatorian of my class, and instead of being thankful for her full tuition scholarship at an Ivy League school, she spent three minutes of her speech talking about how many decimals she was away from valedictorian.

Then I had another friend. We'll name him Mike. Mike was the kind of person who always ended up getting a job that he didn't see coming. The job was a blessing from God at first. When that first paycheck came, you couldn't stop Mike from shouting and preaching and speaking in tongues on his way to his library job. But, the next week, Mike would be applying for another position. Do you know anyone else like Mike? I know 1,000 of these folks—yes, Christian folk. Apparently, Mike had to quit for reasons that made no sense at all. He complained that the vending machine was too far away from the front desk and he complained when his boss didn't say "Hello" loud enough. He complained that his co-workers didn't like him. He complained, he complained, he complained. I wanted to say, "Mike, it's been three days. They don't even know you!" But, of course, if I had said that, I would've become the opposition in his life that he needed to get rid of. So, I kept quiet. And no, Mike hadn't secured another job before leaving the first one. He just simply "stepped out on faith" and trusted God to provide a different job.

My other friend's name is Sharene. She and I attended a funeral together during my junior year. Ironically, she had just finished singing a song titled "I Won't Complain" at the funeral (now why she sang a song about herself at someone else's funeral still eludes me, but anyway)-- then she sat down at the repast and refused to eat because her chicken salad was too cold! Umm Sharene...it's chicken *salad*! And get this. Sharene had enough nerve to ask the hostess to hurry up with the collard greens and sweet tea even after she swore up and down that she wasn't going to eat! A shame, a shame, a shame. Oh...and let's not forget Jose. Jose *always* had a code red emergency. He apparently had five or six grandmothers in his family because every year in high school, another grandmother would die. Conveniently, they all died before final exams.

Now listen.

I'm not trying to judge anyone, but after a few deaths in the family and no evidence of an obituary written up or an address given to send a card to the bereaved, one cannot help but to wonder, "Just how many grandmothers does it take to get to the center of Jose's family tree?" Jose had an enormous excuse issue. He would even complain three weeks after the alleged funerals: "I can't participate in the talent show...I just lost my grandmother," or, "Mr. Johnson, I can't finish my paper until the summer...I just lost my grandmother's grandmother." It was just so much complaining, complaining, complaining. ...

------------◈------------

Complaining is contagious. The more you hang around ungrateful, snobby and always-got-a-problem people, the more you will begin to carry around those same stinky attributes. Before you know it, you'll forget to thank God for all of the things you do have that others do not.

------------◈------------

God: Shaun, quit lying.

Ok, fine Lord! So I can't lie anymore. These friends didn't go to high school with me. Their names weren't Mike, Sally, or Jose.

These friends are shadows of myself.

They are embellished stories that I made up to hide behind my own perfect image. You know how this goes in church. You really want help but are too ashamed to admit that the friend of a friend who's cheating on her husband is you?

Right. This was a bad habit of mine. I would cover up my issues by pointing out someone else's. I could pinpoint on all fingers and toes how many ungrateful Christians I knew, but the biggest of complainers…was me. The narrative below is a true story about how God exposed me to the complainer I never knew existed.

My good friend Lyvonne and I were on the phone one day after class. The conversation began by her asking, "How are you?" It ended with God whispering, "It could've been you…" I was complaining non-stop about my Duke experience. I was only midway into my first semester but I was ready to drop out. The classes weren't fulfilling. My dorm room was really small. The reading assignments were boring. A lot of people looked like me, but very few people *sounded* like me. The paper topics were too abstract. The church history class I wanted to subtract. One of my "Christian" professors I felt needed a salvation tract. And McDonald's wasn't cutting it every night. Blah blah blah. But I didn't stop there. I gave 5,000 more reasons why I needed to leave my Resident Assistant job and find another one because well, the vending machine was too far away—just kidding. But seriously, I started to complain about things that really had no relevance.

Now at the time, I wasn't married. I felt lonely some days. But the friends I met were too needy. Some were too spiritual for me. Oh yeah I said it. Then, my money was a little tight. I needed a new light to match my new comforter set. I didn't like the vacuum cleaner in my dorm so I had to buy my own. And as I was just about to complain about my black microwave not matching with my white refrigerator, I flipped open my laptop and up popped a news flash about poverty. It said, "According to the World Bank, of the worlds 6 billion people, 2.8 billion live on less than $2 a day and 1.2 billion on less than $1 a day."[i] Talk about seeing God in everything. Certainly the Lord shut me up.

[i] "Half the World Lives on Less Than $2 a Day – Brief Article." <u>UN Chronicle</u>. 2000. Gale Group. 7 Apr. 2008
<http://findarticles.com/p/articles/mi_m1309/is_3_37/ai_70654234/>

HAVE A LITTLE TALK WITH JESUS

After reading the statistic on poverty, I quickly ended my earthly conversation in order to have a heavenly one. The moment I bent down to pray, God bombarded me with these convicting words:

God: You've changed a lot since I've talked to you last.

Me: No I haven't.

God: Indeed you have. You've become ungrateful, picky and demanding. You know it's not my custom to throw things up in your face, but I can't let you go another day complaining about things that don't matter. You prayed to go to Duke and I heard your cry. It was Me that softened the heart of the Dean who didn't want to accept your Masters thesis. I pulled you off of the waiting list at Duke and to top it off, I blessed you with a hefty scholarship! That was Me, beloved.

Me: I know, Lord. And I thank you for it, but you know...it's been a rough sem--

God: Seminary is where you told me you wanted to go. I honored *your* prayer and this is the thanks I get? You had nowhere to live in North Carolina. You came down one weekend to rent an apartment and I ordered your steps. I held up a job for you that supplied the housing you needed. You were grateful then, but now...do I hear you complaining? That strange fire of complaint hurts me to the core of my compassionate heart. You must have forgotten that you applied five months after the deadline.

Me: I didn't forget. I just thought I'd own a house by now. I mean, I'm faithful to you...

God: Son, you are beginning to lose focus of the things that really matter. You must really think you are entitled to my grace and favor huh? If you think your "holy" living merits some type of heavenly allowance from me, you're greatly misinformed. Please don't forget, I premiered my greatest love act before you auditioned for the supporting role. While you were yet a sinner, I died. I gave my greatest gift while you were still a layaway item that no one wanted to pay for but everyone wanted to sample. I gave you the finest diamond while you were still a fair cubic zirconia. I gave you Me.

Me: I know, Lord. I didn't mean to—

God: I'm not done, son. Before you joined a church, I died. Before you sang a solo in the young adult choir, I rose. Hmm. A rose. That's what I used to see in you. But every time you complain, your beautiful petals begin to wither away. Pretty soon, I'll be holding a naked flower full of dead memories and prickly thorns. *Ouch. It hurts to hold you now.* Listen to your Life-giver: Don't let that murmuring tongue ruin your beautiful rose. There are many people who have less material wealth than you and yet they praise me for clean water and fresh air. Name the last time you washed in cold water.

Me: I can't.

God: Can you remember a day where you went to sleep hungry?

Me: No.

God: Then what is there to complain about? Look in your closet. Look in your wallet! I love you too much to let you remain this way. When will it stop?

Me: Lord, I don't know how I could've ever been so ungrateful. I'm so sorry.

God: I forgive you. I love you. Go and sin no more. Share with others what happened to you today. Tell the truth, the whole truth, and nothing but the truth. And when you're done, clean up the reputation of me that you've spilt on the floor.

Me: I promise.

OPEN REBUKE IS BETTER THAN SECRET LOVE

Proverbs 27:5 Open rebuke is better than secret love.

The Lord spared no punches and withheld no blows. He let me have it. But the raw truth is, I deserved every bit of it. Let me be candid. On a regular basis I would sing, "I will bless the Lord at all times" during Morning Worship, and in between the 11:00 service and the 3:30, I would be asking God for more of this or more of that. I was a complainer! I was ungrateful. I longed for unnecessary amenities and accessories, when 2.8 billion people live on less than 2 bucks a day. 2 bucks! And you know what? I think some of those people wouldn't trade places with us if they were paid to do so. Why? Because some of the poorest people (financially speaking) have learned contentment and joy in a way that we will never know.

God rebuked me because He loves me. Proverbs 27:5 teaches, "Open rebuke is better than secret love." Hmmm. That's "deep." *Open rebuke is better than secret love.* A really cute proverb, but what exactly does it mean? Well, for starters, it means that your truest friends are those who will confront you openly and respectfully, instead of sitting silently in the corner while others talk about you. It means that your best teachers are those who tell you "this sentence is a run-on" or "that algebraic expression is incorrect," as opposed to giving you an A+ for C- work. Open rebukers are not secret lovers. You see, secret lovers are also secret liars. They will lay down with you tonight and leave you tomorrow. They will lie to get what they want out of you, and once your vending machine has sold out, they will drop you for the latest Pepsi machine around the corner. Secret lovers are also sketchy lovers. They will erase your name off of their chalky sidewalk quicker than dirt can make mud in the rain. An open rebuke, however, indicates transparency and trust. God loved me enough to keep it real. He taught me what it really meant to love my neighbor as myself. Most importantly, He caused me to evaluate those who call themselves my friends. I now know that the ones who love the hardest will sometimes hurt your feelings in order to help your faith. I also know that those who hide their love behind closed doors should expect for me to lock that door, throw away the key, and move on with my life. I don't have time for secret Santa's. I need a straightforward Savior. That's why I love God the way I do. Whenever I get it wrong or if ever my vision gets blurry, God loves me enough to correct my lenses. He wants me to succeed and prosper, and He wants to introduce me to true prosperity. But in order to achieve what God had in store for me, He first had to chasten out my carnal desires and complaining spirit.

-------------◈-------------

Prayer: Lord, I've lost focus.
My vision of you is distorted.
I need your corrective lenses.
Something or someone has
blurred my spiritual sight.
Help me to focus on the things
that really matter. I'm sorry
for complaining. Amen

-------------◈-------------

BECAUSE GOD LOVES YOU, HE'LL SHO'NUFF CHASTEN YOU

Hebrews 12:6 states, "For whom the Lord loveth he chasteneth…" The word *chasten* should not be confused with the word *chasing*. Chasten does not refer to an innocent game of catch and be caught, even though God loves to find us (Luke 15:4).[1] Rather, to be chastened means to be corrected, reproved, taught. *Wow. So why would a loving God discipline us?* Answer: Because He loves us. You see, God's justice, firmness, and steadfast chastening are evidence of His faithful love toward us. The same way a parent reprimands a child, God will sometimes correct us whether we like it or not. But know this: God's chastening is always for our *Christ*ening.

The more Christ-like we become on Earth, the better prepared we are to reign with Christ in heaven.

I can now tell God, "Thank you for the chasing," because God not only rebuked me publically; He also helped me privately. That heavenly rebuke introduced me to one of the nastiest plagues that has come to spoil the harvest of every Christian laborer; that being, the demon of discontentment. People of God, beware of this imp! The demon of discontentment will trick you into buying a house that God never told you to purchase. Discontentment will deceive you into marrying a woman who maybe physically appealing but is inwardly dysfunctional. And yes, we all have our tidbit of dysfunction, but the point is, don't be so quick to run for President with a candidate whom God has not elected. If you base godly decisions solely on the attractiveness of someone's outer coating, it is probably not a godly decision. All throughout the Bible we see God honoring substance over style and the anointing over the aesthetic. This is precisely why we need to be delivered from discontentment. Discontentment is the proud son of delusion and the grandson of deception. If we're ever going to make spiritual changes in our city, country, or world, we've got to branch onto a different family tree, repent of our ungratefulness, and learn to be content.

LEARNING TO BE CONTENT

Philippians 4:11 Not that I speak in respect of want: for I have learned in whatsoever state I am, therewith to be content.

Numbers 11:1 And when the people complained, it displeased the Lord: and the Lord heard it; and his anger was kindled; and the fire of the Lord burnt among them, and consumed them that were in the uttermost parts of the camp.

I listed these Scriptures at the beginning of this chronicle for a reason. If you really want to stop complaining, these are two verses you should know and understand. In Philippians, Paul is writing a letter to the church at Philippi from prison. He is in prison, friends. Not because he murdered anyone or because he forgot to pay child support. Paul was imprisoned because he had become a servant of righteousness (Romans 6:19).[2] *Wow.* Isn't it interesting? Paul (whose former name was Saul) had persecuted Christians before Christ (Acts 9:1),[3] but wasn't thrown into prison until after becoming an evangelist for Christ. Paul is in prison, and not only that, he is awaiting his death sentence. He expects to die pretty soon, but while he waits for that final curtain call, Paul decides to practice what he has learned. In whatsoever state he is in, he will be content.

If you allow your mind to wallow in the dark pools of complaint, you will drown out each and every blessing God has floating above the water.

Every once in a while, stick your head out of the waters of sadness, pity, and complaint. Inhale the oxygen God has provided. Even oxygen is an undeserved blessing that we often take for granted.

He is so content that he tells his guards about Jesus (Philippians 1:12-14).[4] Eventually, the guards get bored with this crazy man's testimony, so Paul switches audiences and starts encouraging other Christians. He tells the church to "stand fast in the Lord" (Philippians 4:1)[5] even though he is confined to a prison cell. He is in the middle of his darkest night, and yet he's still walking in the light. Can you imagine what it must have been like to be Paul at this point? I certainly can't. I think I would've been writing—*I mean, there really isn't much to do in jail*— but, I don't think I would be encouraging anyone, that's for sure. The moment someone told me I would be put to death for believing in God, my Christian days of encouragement would've been over. You probably think I'm joking, but I'm quite serious. I can see my final chapter now…creatively titled: "You've Gotta Be Kiddin' Me! Get Me Outta Here!" But no, instead of denying Christ, giving up, or writing a sloppy shorthand letter to his lawyer, Paul begins a new chapter titled, "Final Days: Learning

Contentment." He writes, I imagine, after looking around to a cold and bare cell. There are no pillows for comfort. There is no family picture to clutch onto. There are no microphones, stage lights, or cute little juice glasses from which to drink his final beverage. Of all the things to say, Paul scribbles, "I have learned to be content."

Learned. Hmmm. That word alone strikes me as a simple yet profound verb choice. Paul did not just wake up one morning and know how contentment worked. No one wakes up in the morning with contentment on the brain. Contentment doesn't just magically happen. Paul had to learn contentment. The same way we learn to tie our shoes, balance a checkbook, recite the ABC's, or memorize the books of the Bible, Paul chose to put into practice what he had learned, and best of all, Paul didn't depend on a crowd of onlookers to persuade him to the left or to the right. In the same way, we've got to learn how to be content in the prison, in the palace, in the shelter, or in the sanctuary. Singles, don't allow your marital status to get in the way of your praise and worship. Practice contentment. It could be a lot worse. Employees, you must choose to be content with your job even if you are overworked and underpaid. Learn contentment. It could be a lot worse. Life occupants, learn to be content with that which God has blessed you. Life, even as a Christian, is all about making choices and living with them. Life doesn't hand you a first aid kit during an emergency, and neither does the church. That's our problem. Too many of us are disappointed in God because we ran to Him for a quick fix and not because He was our Father.

We treated God like He was only good enough to be our Hospitalist (our emergency doctor) instead of our Primary Care Physician. We would love for God to just prescribe a get-better-quick church that will make us feel good about life, but the truth is, this is twisted theology. God is much more than a "get out of jail" free card. God is not like the tooth fairy who places dollars under our pillow every time we lose a tooth. No, God is God, and this Christian journey will require us to learn and practice contentment! If someone taught you that knowing Christ meant you would never have to practice contentment, they have lied to you. Christians endure tough times, rough times and even the New York Times by choosing contentment over complaint.

There are plenty Christians who claim to know Christ but are still dissatisfied with life's outcome. Paul was so satisfied with knowing Christ that he witnessed and worshiped in the middle of his wilderness! The book of Numbers, on the other hand, tells of another group of followers who did not worship during rough times. They were called "the chosen people of God" but they were whimperers and whiners. God had delivered them out of Egyptian bondage, and still, they complained. God would provide a cloud by day, fire by night and some manna from heaven to eat. No, it wasn't steak, eggs, or a house salad; but it was food. And instead of being grateful, they complained to Moses about their present situation and begged for fish, cucumbers, and melon (Numbers 11:5).[6] So delusional did they become, that they contemplated returning back to captivity just to guzzle down a #2 from McDonald's extra value meal.

Had the Israelites learned what Paul had put into practice, they would have been able to see God in the manna. But, unfortunately, they didn't know how to control their complaining. So, God responded harshly. The Bible says, "His anger was kindled; and the fire of the Lord burnt among them and consumed them that were in the uttermost parts of the camp" (Numbers 11:1).[7] But before destroying them all, you know what God did? He gave them what they asked for.

In verse 20, God promised to give so much meat that it eventually came out from their nostrils! *Yuck!* Moses thought God was kidding, but in verse 32, the people gathered the quail (God provided enough quail to feed over 600,000 people) and everyone who ate this meat got sick. Then, when they finished their food, God pronounced a benediction over their lives (Numbers 11:33).[8] Read it for yourself! It's right there in the book of Numbers.

God doesn't take well to those who complain even after He provides. Your situation may seem a bit dim and unfortunate, but if you look around, you've got some evidence of manna in your life. Find the manna and bury the memory. If you let memories run your life, it will ruin your tomorrow. What you're being served today might not taste like the meat you once loved, but it sure is better than being enslaved to something you know God never intended. So, the choice is really yours. Which kind of Christian will you be? Will you be a complainer or will you practice contentment? Again, contentment does not happen overnight. Don't trick yourself into expecting microwave results. It is a learned behavior and you've got to decide to be content.

------------ ◈ ------------

Do you know any ungrateful children who complain about old computers or slow internet? If so, direct them to the book of Numbers. I'm sure if you explain how some of the Israelites lost their lives getting what they never needed, they'll change their mind about that new X-box. I do not mean threaten the kid. But, teach them to appreciate the manna blessings.

------------ ◈ ------------

GODLINESS WITH CONTENTMENT IS GREAT GAIN

1 Timothy 6:6-8 But godliness with contentment is great gain. For we brought nothing into this world, and it is certain we can carry nothing out. And having food and raiment let us be therewith content.

1 Timothy 6:9-10 But they that will be rich fall into temptation and a snare, and into many foolish and hurtful lusts, which drown men in destruction and perdition. For the love of money is the root of all evil: which while some coveted after, they have erred from the faith, and pierced themselves through with many sorrows.

I know we would rather stick in a set of invisible earplugs, but the reality is, we can't pretend these verses don't exist.

Contentment is important. Contentment keeps our motive pure. It is the spiritual accountant that makes sure our donations and accomplishments do not become baby idols in our garden of success. The above Scripture does not simply say godliness is great gain. It says godliness *with contentment* is great gain. Why is contentment a key component of our gain? Quite simply, because contentment is the weighing scale that helps us to balance who we are. Contentment is like Vitamin C for every Christian who aspires to be spiritually healthy. We need contentment because this Christian walk is more of a tightrope balance than it is a walk in the park. Contentment will train the carnal mind not to be frustrated if the thing you're reaching for is too high for you to grab right now. Contentment is that supernatural power that every shopaholic needs in order to say, "No! I don't need another pair of shoes today." Even the college student needs a pinch of contentment so she will not end up in credit card debt for the rest of her life after the party season has ended. Contentment helps us realize what we are already fortunate enough to have.

Fortunate enough to have. What a wonderful way to bring up my next point! I think the primary reason some of us cannot reap the benefits of God's blessing is because we don't recognize them. We are fortunate, and don't even realize it. We have a well functioning car, but we complain if we don't have a car like the pastor. We don't recognize our blessing until we become the worker without transportation. We don't appreciate the blessings until we have to wake up at 5 AM to arrive at a job that other people (who have cars) drag into twenty minutes late. It was just three months ago when we said, "Lord, just give me a job. Just give me one more chance to get it right. Just let me get accepted into that program." And by the next page of our comic strip, God finds us hunched over the desk, hands burying our face, and complaining until we go to church. Once we get there, instead of repenting for our ungratefulness, we run around screaming, "The Lord is going to give me a new job!! I'm walking in my new season!" *Ouch.* And don't get me wrong. God may give you a new job. But how about you show God appreciation for the one you have before you lay out demands for the one you think you need?

WE THINK WE ARE ENTITLED TO GOD'S BENEVOLENCE

Romans 12:1 I beseech you therefore, brethren, by the mercies of God, that ye present your bodies a living sacrifice, holy, acceptable unto God, [which is] your reasonable service.

If there is anything worse than having nothing, it is having more than enough and asking God for a surplus without proper cause. We get accepted into school, and then we want out. Why?—Because we need more. We pray for medical insurance, and God blesses us with it; then we stop going to the doctor. Why?—Because we want someone else to pay our insurance premium. When the pressure gets turned up on our business God gave us, we want to take down the sign and start over. We give fewer things and still we ask for more. No matter how much God blesses us with, and no matter how much we achieve, we're never satisfied. Do you think God is pleased with our commotion and complaint? I'm certain that He is not.

There is something in the air that is far worse than H1N1. It is simply called entitlement. Oh yeah. That's the last relative I forgot to mention. Discontentment has a first cousin whose name is entitlement. And entitlement has a daddy. His name is Ego. If you are known to complain about little things, then you're probably caught up in who you think you are and what you think you deserve. That's what entitlement will do to you. It will con you into believing that you deserve more from God than others (like your unsaved family members or co-workers) simply because you give money to feed homeless children; when the Scripture clearly states: "He maketh his sun to rise on the evil and on the good, and sendeth rain on the just and on the unjust" (Matthew 5:45).[9] I know this is a hard pill to swallow but we've got to hear the truth. We owe God far more than God owes us.

Once upon a time, Calvary was enough. Once upon a time, the blood Jesus shed was sufficient. But now we have entered a dispensation of ungratefulness and entitlement. We live as if God owes us something. God doesn't owe you a house, a car, or a husband simply because you've presented your body as a living sacrifice. Holy living is our reasonable service (Romans 12:1).[10] In other words, this is minimum wage. It is the least we can do for God. What God desires from us is far greater than our net worth. He wants us to know Him, not just to tolerate Him. To trust Him, not just to believe that He "exists." To lean on Him, not just factor Him into our lives during seasons of desperation or grief. Let it be said here if it is not said anywhere else: We are not doing God a favor by serving Him. We are certainly not helping His mission if we're murmuring and complaining under our breath. We've got to get delivered from entitlement. We can't live another day like this. And maybe then, after God has turned us away from our own selfish desires, we will understand the pain God feels when He constantly gives and we continually beg for more.

GRAB A MOP AND CLEAN GOD'S REPUTATION

How would you like it if the only time someone entered your house, they came with their hand out expecting you to bless them, give to them, pamper them, serve them? When are we as the church going to bless God (Psalm 34:1),[11] give to God (Psalm 29:2),[12] pamper God (John 11:2),[13] serve God (Psalm 100:2)?[14] You think God doesn't desire our pampering? You think God's reputation doesn't need fixing? As poorly as we have represented God, I think we should take on the responsibility of cleaning up the mess we've made. We are the ones God will use to get the house back in order. I'm not going to sit around and wait for another Moses to tell me what God has already revealed. We are called to worship until God's heart heals from the misuse, abuse and disorderly conduct we've caused. Remember, it was the pain of a broken heart that caused God to wipe out Noah's generation. It was the disappointment of a relational God that dismissed Adam and Eve from the garden but still clothed them and made sure they were safe in the wilderness of their own wandering. It was righteous anger that caused God to rebuke those who turned the house of prayer into a den of thieves (Luke 19:46).[15] Jesus saves the woman caught in adultery, but He also leaves her with one condition: go and sin no more (John 8:11).[16] I believe He is calling us to do the same. At some point in our Christian journey, we've got to stop complaining and start cleaning up the reputation that we've spilt on the floor. A lot of people won't come to church because we don't reflect God's attitude. We barely speak in a manner that sounds like God. Let's be real. Christ wasn't a complainer. Christ was a healer. He healed a multitude of people immediately after receiving word that his friend Lazarus had died. Who have you healed with your words? Jesus was content with a little so that we could be blessed with much. Jesus never owned a home and never got married. He was content. He was persecuted for our sins and criticized for our guiltiness; of all people, Jesus had the right to complain. But instead of complaining, He reached out his bloodied hands and whispered, "Father, forgive them. For they know not what they do" (Luke 23:34).[17]

WHAT IS THERE TO COMPLAIN ABOUT?

Hebrews 13:5 Let your conversation be without covetousness; and be content with such things as ye have: for he hath said, I will never leave thee, nor forsake thee.

Let this chronicle be a lesson to us all. Instead of sowing seed for a new house, learn to be content with the apartment. As you believe God for a new job, thank God for the one you have. If you're unemployed, use your free time to serve the lesser fortunate. You may be contemplating divorce because you feel like you've married the wrong guy, but instead of complaining, how about you spend more time meditating on God's promises? God promised never to leave you (Hebrews 13:5).[18] He promised to renew your strength if you would be willing to wait (Isaiah 40:31).[19] He promised to be a very present help in the time of trouble (Psalm 46:1).[20]   If you meditate on God's promises, you will eventually stumble up on the purpose behind your problem. Perhaps your husband's deliverance will come if you just hang in there for a little while longer and work through the fiery trials. *Learn to be content.*

Take control of your complaining tendency before it destroys your entire outlook on life. The Israelites were so hungry for meat in Egypt that many of them forfeited milk, honey, and the Promised Land. Don't let your tummy direct your trust in God. If discontentment tries to blur your vision, wipe off your windshield wipers with a little "I'm grateful" fluid. Take a walk down memory lane and thank God for the many blessings we so easily take for granted. In fact, let's do that right now. Let me name seven simple things that God has done for us. Sometimes, all we need is a good reminder:

- ❖ God has protected you from car accident after car accident. Even the accidents you witnessed or were affected by, God spared you for a reason and you are still alive to tell the story.
- ❖ God sustained your breathing while you slept last night. He can surely keep you alive while you are awake.
- ❖ Most of us have never seen a day where we had to sit outside and beg for money in front of a fast food restaurant.
- ❖ Remember that time you forgot to turn off the stove, or you left the iron on all day? Somehow, your house was not ablaze when you returned. And if it was, are you still homeless? Did God not provide for you?
- ❖ You are walking around on two very good legs. If you can't walk, then maybe you can talk. If you can't talk, then maybe you have two eyes. Your worst day this year was someone else's best day ever.
- ❖ God has introduced you to people who have made a permanent impact on your life. These people are so important to you now, you can't envision your life without them.

❖ While you were yet a sinner, Christ died.

Are you convinced yet? Do you see why there is no real reason to complain about anything? I hope so. I hope this chronicle has caused you to reflect over your life and decide contentment over complaint. Whatever you're murmuring about, I dare you to find the closest scale and weigh your issues next to all of life's benefits. You'll discover, just like I did, that God has truly been good to you.

Questions for Introspection

ᑎ_____ᔕ

1) Has the complaining stopped for you yet? If not, think of five reasons to be grateful and meditate on those reasons for the next few days. Then, imagine life without those five, and find another five things to be grateful for. Go on…do it!

2) Perhaps God wants to use what you are going through as a means to minister to others. Can you pull anything out of your unfortunate situation that might help to transform someone else's life?

Practical Points

ᑎ_____ᔕ

1 If you ever find yourself on the verge of complaining, volunteer at the nearest homeless shelter or sign up at a hospital to do some volunteer work. Better yet, drive two towns over to a different neighborhood and just sit down and learn. There is really nothing to complain about. God is with you and He is more than enough.

2 Remember, Paul was in prison and was facing death. He not only found time to learn contentment, but he found the strength to encourage the church. Learn how to take control over your mind, and begin to speak contentment to your spirit. I know it sounds funny, but say aloud "I am content. I am learning to be content." This will keep you from overlooking the blessings you already have.

3 Maybe your cloud of complaint is blocking the sunray of God's blessing. We make our lives all the more problematic when we complain. If you can't afford gifts for Christmas, don't complain—just don't buy any. There will be plenty more December 25th's.

4 Learning contentment in a world filled with temptation (money, success, and beautiful bodies) is no easy lesson to master. But, the Master behind the message, Jesus Christ, can help with every predicament you could ever face. Just start practicing contentment day by day, and pretty soon, you'll get a handle on the solution as opposed to having life's problem handle you.

5 Contentment does not give you permission to get lazy and never take risks. Be content with what God has blessed you with, but at the same time, don't settle for anything less than what God has promised. I am personally not content with unsaved family members. You shouldn't be either. I am not content with writing one book when I know God has equipped me to write ten. There's a fine line between contentment and complacency.

Scripture Glossary

[1]**Luke 15:4** *What man of you, having an hundred sheep, if he lose one of them, doth not leave the ninety and nine in the wilderness, and go after that which is lost, until he find it?*

[2]**Romans 6:19** *I speak after the manner of men because of the infirmity of your flesh: for as ye have yielded your members servants to uncleanness and to iniquity unto iniquity; even so now yield your members servants to righteousness unto holiness.*

[3]**Acts 9:1** *And Saul, yet breathing out threatenings and slaughter against the disciples of the Lord, went unto the high priest.*

[4]**Philippians 1:12-14** *But I would ye should understand, brethren, that the things which happened unto me have fallen out rather unto the furtherance of the gospel; So that my bonds in Christ are manifest in all the palace, and in all other places; And many of the brethren in the Lord, waxing confident by my bonds, are much more bold to speak the word without fear.*

[5]**Philippians 4:1** *Therefore, my brethren dearly beloved and longed for, my joy and crown, so stand fast in the Lord, my dearly beloved.*

[6]**Numbers 11:5** *We remember the fish, which we did eat in Egypt freely; the cucumbers, and the melons, and the leeks, and the onions, and the garlick.*

[7]**Numbers 11:1** *And when the people complained, it displeased the LORD: and the LORD heard it; and his anger was kindled; and the fire of the LORD burnt among them, and consumed them that were in the uttermost parts of the camp.*

[8]**Numbers 11:33** *And while the flesh was yet between their teeth, ere it was chewed, the wrath of the LORD was kindled against the*

people, and the LORD smote the people with a very great plague.

[9]**Matthew 5:45** *That ye may be the children of your Father which is in heaven: for he maketh his sun to rise on the evil and on the good, and sendeth rain on the just and on the unjust.*

[10]**Romans 12:1** *I beseech you therefore, brethren, by the mercies of God, that ye present your bodies a living sacrifice, holy, acceptable unto God, which is your reasonable service.*

[11]**Psalm 34:1** *I will bless the LORD at all times: his praise shall continually be in my mouth.*

[12]**Psalm 29:2** *Give unto the LORD the glory due unto his name; worship the LORD in the beauty of holiness.*

[13]**John 11:2** *(It was that Mary which anointed the Lord with ointment, and wiped his feet with her hair, whose brother Lazarus was sick.)*

[14]**Psalm 100:2** *Serve the LORD with gladness: come before his presence with singing.*

[15]**Luke 19:46** *Saying unto them, It is written, My house is the house of prayer: but ye have made it a den of thieves.*

[16]**John 8:11** *She said, No man, Lord. And Jesus said unto her, Neither do I condemn thee: go, and sin no more.*

[17]**Luke 23:34** *Then said Jesus, Father, forgive them; for they know not what they do. And they parted his raiment, and cast lots.*

[18]**Hebrews 13:5** *Let your conversation be without covetousness; and be content with such things as ye have: for he hath said, I will never leave thee, nor forsake thee.*

[19]**Isaiah 40:31** *But they that wait upon the LORD shall renew their strength; they shall mount up with wings as eagles; they shall run,*

and not be weary; and they shall walk, and not faint.

[20]**Psalm 46:1** *God is our refuge and strength, a very present help in trouble.*

CHRONICLES THAT *EXAMINE*

ೞ_____ೞ

ENDORSING A CHECK

Does God Recognize His Signature in your Life?

cx_____so

Looking unto Jesus the author and finisher of our faith...
Hebrews 12:2

*[H]aving this seal, the Lord knoweth them that are his. And, let every one that nameth the name of Christ **depart** from iniquity.*
2 Timothy 2:19

*Not every one that saith unto me, Lord, Lord, shall enter into the kingdom of heaven; but he that doeth the will of my Father which is in heaven. **Many will say** to me in that day, Lord, Lord, have we not prophesied in thy name? and in thy name have cast out devils? and in thy name done many wonderful works? And then will I profess unto them, I never knew you: **depart** from me, ye that work iniquity.*
Matthew 7:21-23

*A*fter I learned to write cursive letters in elementary school, the first thing I wanted to master was my signature. I wanted to create an iconic autograph; one that no one else could duplicate. I must say, in the utmost humility, I think I succeeded. My signature has character. My signature has umph! If you look at all of the documents from elementary school until now, you'll be able to identify me because it's distinguishable from the simple left to right signatures. Instead of writing two S letters for my first and last name, I make one big S and place the –haun on top of the –aunders. It has a swooped H in the middle of Shaun Saunders and no one can swoop that H, in my opinion, quite like me. Trust me. It's one of coolest signatures you'll ever see!

You know, signatures are really important nowadays. A

signature on paper is all you need to seal a contractual agreement. It verifies who agreed to what, and it is the primary reason why enlisted soldiers cannot say, "Oops. I made a mistake. I want to go home." Sallie Mae and bill collectors will call and call and call (they will even call your cell phone) until you pay back college loans and credit cards, all because of your signature.

Well one day, I went to the bank to deposit a check. I filled out the deposit slip in the car and was ready to get my money! I walked in. The bank was flooded with people. *Just great. The last place I want to spend my entire Saturday afternoon is at the bank.* I stood in that long line like an antsy youngster inching toward the newest rollercoaster. I tried my best to be patient. *Why were people so slow?* Sigh. *Won't they just hurry up?* Finally, the red sign flashed: TELLER AVAILABLE. I briskly rushed over to the banker and thrust my check and deposit slip under the glass. The teller looked at my check, turned it around, and pushed it back nastily.

"I'm sorry sir. I can't deposit this. It doesn't have your signature," she said.

What? The aggravation began. *Don't panic. Just get a pen.* I reached into my pocket. I had a pen! *Awesome Jesus!* I leaned down to sign the check and the pen didn't work! *Not so awesome, Jesus.* Aggravated and tired, I begged the person behind me for a pen. She gave it to me and of course hers didn't work either. So like a whiny little baby, I slithered out of the line. Someone took my place. I stomped over to the welcome table, signed the check, and what do you know? I had to go to the end of the line and start all over again.

Has this ever happened to you before? If so, I'm sure you agree—it is really frustrating when you need to sign something and the ink doesn't work. I didn't want to see God in this, but I couldn't help it. As I stood in the back of the line, God whispered, "If I am the author of your faith, then why can't I see My signature in your life?"

JESUS: THE BEST-~~SELLING~~ LIVING AUTHOR EVER!
Hebrews 12:2 ...Jesus the author...

Many of us are like the unsigned check I brought into the bank that day. We have money, we've earned a few degrees, and we boast in our profession or success, and still, we have no value without Jesus. We exist but we really aren't living. We breathe but we really aren't alive. We have no clue why we are here and no definition to life. We just play out a bunch of roles. We are unsigned checks waiting for someone to assume authorship over our lives. Hebrews tells us who the author should be—Jesus Christ—but, most people (even in the church) don't really know who Jesus is. It was Jesus who instituted change in our world, not President Obama. It was Jesus who recovered our totaled vehicles of life and engineered us back into mobility. He helped us when we were helpless and gave us hope when we were hopeless. This is, as the blind man put it, "*that* man who is called Jesus," (John 9:11).[1] This same Jesus authored humanity's story into *His*-story long before pens were invented and humans were created; and He died, rose, and ascended so our end could read "happily ever after" instead of "hell ever after." It was Jesus who filled our pen with the ink of a unique purpose, and became "the author of eternal salvation unto all them that obey him" (Hebrews 5:9).[2] His credentials exceed any earthly occupation and His foolishness is wiser than man's wisdom (1 Corinthians 1:25).[3] If Jesus ain't qualified to author your life, let me be the first to tell you, no one else is. He created you to do much more with Him than you could ever do without Him. And I can't speak for you, but I don't want to ever live without Him! Life without Jesus' authorship is no life at all. Without Jesus, you'll become as a city that is broken down and without walls (Proverbs 25:28).[4] Without Jesus, you might become a church member but you can't become a heaven member (John 14:6).[5] Without Jesus, we're just actors on a stage, like a child who's lost his way, and we wouldn't be here today without Him (thanks Kirk Franklin).

Why give God author-ity to author my life? Quite simply, because He's the best-living author ever! God knows you better than you know yourself. He knows your fast-forward better than you know your rewind. He knows how much money you'll have in the bank on the day you die, and He even knows how many hairs are on your head (Luke 12:7).[6] God knows how many books you have on the bookshelf that you have yet to read, yet He sees you run to the bookstore and splurge on new ones anyway (don't act like I'm the only one). God knows more and wants to teach you all things (John 14:26).[7] Best of all, God wants to introduce you to the best *you* anyone has ever seen!

----------◇----------
Lord: I don't think I really know who I am. I know You desire to use me, but I keep running out of ink. My life is leaking. My soul is fainting. Please author my life. Amen.
----------◇----------

IS MY LIFE PREPARED FOR THE HEAVENLY DEPOSIT?

Hebrews 12:2 ...and finisher of our faith

No matter how angelic our voices are, and no matter how big our churches become, we all need to ask ourselves, "Is my life officially prepared for the heavenly deposit?" I don't want to get to heaven, stand in line, and discover when I get to the front "window" that God cannot deposit my soul into the bank of everlasting life. When all is said and done, I want God to endorse my tenure here on Earth. Yes, I said endorse. That's a fancy word used to describe the process of signing a check. You see, I don't just want to be a good person. Good people go to hell, too (Romans 3:23).[8] Nor do I *just* want to be religious; for the Scriptures declare, "if the righteous scarcely be saved, where shall the ungodly and the sinner appear?" (1 Peter 4:18).[9] No. That's not enough for me. I want to be good, I want to be saved, and I want to be *endorsed*. You see, once a check is endorsed, it is officially prepared for deposit. No matter how many dollars the check represents, no matter how pretty the check is, and no matter how many hours you've been waiting in line, the check can serve no purpose without a signature. It's the law. So, if a check can serve no monetary purpose without a signature, certainly it is possible to live a good life on Earth and still miss heaven without God's endorsement.

God is ready to accept us into His loving care, but are you ready to hear God's final answer? Is your life officially prepared for its heavenly deposit? This is the question I am learning to ask myself daily. Why? Because life is so unpredictable, and most people have no idea when they are going to die. Many preachers don't preach about it until funerals, but death is real. You can be alive one minute and dead the next. The Bible describes life as "a vapor that appears for a little time and then vanishes away" (James 4:14).[10] It would do us all well, then, to live everyday on purpose and pattern ourselves after Jesus so there is no question about our eternal home address.

According to Hebrews 12:2, God is not just the author of our faith, He is the finisher of our faith as well. Please understand: God cares about every single stage of your life. He waves that black and white checkered flag to start your engines and He's holding up a bloodstained banner at the finished line. All along the way, He's coordinating your water breaks, tying your shoes, handing you a towel for relief, and finishing the final stretch with you. He's ever present (Psalm 46:1),[11] yet He stands before us and after us to encourage His racers to sprint a little faster, trust Him a little more, and pray without ceasing. God is a finisher (John 4:34).[12] God is not like most of us who begin a project and never complete it (Luke 14:30).[13] He begins a good work and finishes what He starts (Philippians 1:6).[14] Because God is a finisher, God wants to see you finish! He wants to see you conquer and achieve. Jesus died so you could experience the abundant life and eternal life (John 10:10).[15] He wants to author your life and finish your faith. He really does. But, you must be willing to give him the pen.

WHO HAS THE PEN: JESUS OR SIN?

Hebrews 12:1 ...Let us lay aside every weight, and the sin which doth so easily beset us, and let us run with patience the race that is set before us.

Isaiah 59:2 But your iniquities have separated between you and your God, and your sins have hid his face from you, that he will not hear.

If God can't see His signature on your life, it's probably because something is blocking the Son-Light from your true value and worth. If we ask the prophet Isaiah or the writer of Hebrews, they would both agree: God's view of you is blurred by the blotches of a leaking pen called sin. None of us want to admit it, but the truth is, oftentimes, sin blocks us from completing our God-given assignment. Sin stands in between God and us like a coffin in the middle of a wedding reception. Sin is an ugly little monster whose main purpose is to manufacture death (Romans 6:23).[16] Once sin has captivated your mind and once you have bought into the lies, schemes, and deceptive distractions, you can be convinced out of the will of God (James 1:15).[17] Sin tries to define you by all of the characteristics that God abhors (Proverbs 6:16-19).[18] God sees you as beautiful and capable. Sin tells you are ugly and defeated. God sees you as a conquering soldier and a compassionate friend. Sin sees you as a cowardly lion and a chronic foe. Sin's best sermons are on constant rotation: the church is your enemy and you will never defeat Goliath. God still sees the better, bigger you. God cultivates the gardener in you and communicates to you through dreams. Sin will keep you awake at night and send doubt and distraction in the morning. But if you give Jesus the pen, you can be free from all sin (Romans 8:2).[19]

Please, please hear me. You cannot allow doubt and distraction to block you from God's prepared blessings. Every time you allow the diabolical twins of doubt and distraction to stop up your pen, you stay back another year in spiritual kindergarten. This was the problem with the children of Israel. They turned an 11-day journey into a forty year long merry-go-down (Deuteronomy 1:2).[20] They allowed doubt and distraction to stop them from moving forward, and that's exactly what sin will try to do. Don't let sin steal your pen! The greater you allow sin to build up in your life, the higher the mountain and the steeper the ditch becomes, ultimately creating more and more distance between you and your Author. In the end, one chapter sounds totally disconnected from the rest of the book, all because sin has stolen the pen out of your hand. Sin will try to psych you into believing that God isn't real. Sin is attracted to your weaknesses and desires to pull you out from the soils of God's holiness garden. Sin is a mess! And we are surrounded by a world polluted with it.

DEPARTURE FROM SIN KEEPS THE INK IN THE PEN

2 Timothy 2:19 …[H]aving this seal, the Lord knoweth them that are his. And let every one that nameth the name of Christ **depart** from iniquity.

Psalm 37:27 Depart from evil, and do good; and dwell for evermore.

So, how does one stay holy? How does one refrain from this strong and existent force? What does one do after he or she has given himself to the temptations of flesh? Quick Answer: If you really want God to flow through you freely (on a continual basis), you've got to depart from sin. Departure from sin keeps the ink in the pen. 2 Timothy 2:19 says, "And let every one that nameth the name of Christ depart from iniquity." In other words, ye that work iniquity, depart. Ye who have been hired by sin to be her slave, escape (Romans 6:17-18).[21] Ye who are captivated by the hypnotic of fleshly pleasure, resist (James 4:7).[22] Those whom sin has blinded your mind (2 Corinthians 4:4),[23] open your eyes and run to the nearest holy rehabilitation center for mind renewal. We must depart from those things that gratify us temporarily so that Christ can satisfy us eternally. 1 Thessalonians 5:22 instructs us to abstain from all appearance of evil. If we name the name of Christ, that means we know God. To know God is to love God and to demonstrate our love toward God, we must depart from sin. It's an inevitable step toward true relationship with Jesus Christ. The departure chapters may not be written on the same page for everyone, but every Christian has a date with departure (when he or she decides to change in order to live according to the will of God). Saul, for example, did not write the epistles. Paul did. His moment of departure and conversion occurred on the road to Damascus (Acts 9:3-5).[24] Conversion experiences mark a moment of departure and change. And just like Paul, if you make a decision to depart from iniquity today, you won't think the same tomorrow. You won't desire to do the same things, you won't want to disappoint God, and most importantly, God will be with you to lead you to all truth (John 16:13; Matthew 7:13-14). [25-26] Like it or not, according to the Word of God, we are going to confront departure. Either we depart from iniquity on Earth now, or we depart from God in heaven later.

----------- ◈ -----------

Deliverer, I'm tired of the circular motion. I feel so distant from You and I don't know how to fix this. I really messed up but I'm pleading with You for forgiveness. Forgive me for allowing sin to separate us. Forgive me for losing focus. I want to depart from these areas of darkness in my life, but I need Your help to keep me free. I'm running out of this so I can run into You. Help.

----------- ◈ -----------

RUN AND LOOK…LOOK AND LIVE

Hebrews 12:2 Looking unto Jesus…

Romans 8:13 For if ye live after the flesh, ye shall die: but if ye through the Spirit do mortify the deeds of the body, ye shall live.

We're back to our first highlighted Scripture, but I need to detour your attention for one second. Many people have given Jesus the pen, departed from iniquity, and still feel defeated. They still feel purposeless and they still end up in the long line of unresolved issues, asking the question, "Now what?" Well, the preceding Scripture in Hebrews 12 encourages us to "run with patience the race that is set before us" (Hebrews 12:1).[27] And like Forrest Gump, you've got to keep on running until heaven calls you home (2 Timothy 4:7).[28] Like I said earlier, a heavenly promise is available to us all (Acts 2:39; Hebrews 9:15), [29-30] but in order to have it, we've got to flee from familiar territory and run as fast as we can into God. Running is not a cowardly thing. It is a necessary directive in order to maintain our spiritual health. *Run, Christian, run!* Running is one of Scripture's remedies to us. Standing is too (Ephesians 6:13),[31] but many of us don't like to run. We'll stand all day if there is a little bit of shade or if we can lean on something, but running? Oh no! That's too challenging a task. It requires too much initiative, action, movement, and response. Above all else, in order to run the right way, you've got to look in the direction you are running toward. Yes, I said it-- look where you're running. It sounds simple, but I know too many loved ones who have either run into poles, crashed into parked cars, or collided into glass doors simply because they weren't looking forward. They all ended up in the hospital.

Listen closely, friends. It is possible to run so hard out of a situation that you forget to look forward and you end up back in the pit from which you just escaped. It is possible to be in such a rush to get to church that you miss Jesus on the corner. As a result, you end up bumping into poles or crashing into parked cars, and staying overnight in hospitals just so God can reroute your attention to the things that matter most to Him. Have you ever been there? Cool. So have I. This is the point: Authoring is good, and departing is even better, but after you have done all of that, you've got to look while running. Where you look will determine how you live. What you look upon will influence how you see the world. It would be really hard to run with your head hung down. You can't keep beating yourself up about the things in the past. Old things are passed away (2 Corinthians 5:17).[32] You've got to look unto Jesus. Tie your shoelaces and get back onto the racetrack. I know you've fallen, but get back up again and look unto Jesus (Proverbs 24:16).[33] I know your body isn't up for another lap, but keep your eye on the prize and press toward the mark (Philippians 3:14).[34] Stop relying on feelings to determine your participation in this Christian race. Look unto Jesus! That is where your strength comes from. David wrote, "I will lift up mine eyes to the hills from whence cometh my help" (Psalm 121:1),[35] not because the hills were a great support system, but because of the One who sits high above the hills! Jesus was his help. Take your cue from David and look to Jesus!

It might seem like a minor detail to some, but looking is a major variable in the race equation. You'd be surprised to know how many people try and run this race without looking in the direction of Jesus. They seek out a human counselor before they look to the Wonderful Counselor (Isaiah 9:6).[36] They reach for a psychic hotline before they call Jesus on the mainline. They trust C.N.N. more than G.O.D.; the facts of life more than the Holy Bible. Take it from a boy who has actually gone to church, heard the sermon, and still continued down the wrong path. It pays to look up.

WHAT HAPPENS WHEN GOD LOOKS DOWN?

Psalm 53:2-3 God looked down from heaven upon the children of men, to see if there were any that did understand, that did seek God. Every one of them is gone back: they are altogether become filthy; there is none that doeth good, no, not one.

It pays to look up. Yes. But, what happens when God looks down? What happens when God stands in line behind all of the idols we've placed before Him, waiting for us to signal to Him: TELLER AVAILABLE. What happens when God reaches into His pocket for a pen, only to find that none of His Christian refills are functioning properly anymore? What happens when God's message is not spread because the human bread is stale and infected? What happens when God looks down?

If God were anything like the frustrated customer I had become in the bank that day, I can picture Him walking over toward heaven's desk to write. He's huffing and puffing. He peaks down over creation and scratches off a few lines. He looks at the wayward church, and balls up the paper. He tries to keep silent but realizes His silence must be broken or else His people will be destroyed. After snapping about twelve pencils, He quickly scribbles:

Dearly Beloved:

I can't lie. What you're thinking is me is totally not. I'm not the father of that stage performance you call church. I never signed that. I never endorsed this pastor. I never called that prophet (Matthew 7:15).[37] I don't even know his phone number. Every time I send someone to tell them that I never called them, they ignore my warning and call the true prophet, false and the false prophet, true. I didn't want them to find out like this. But now they come to heaven and I must tell them the truth. I love you too much to allow you to walk around in error. I care too much to sit quietly and watch my beautiful servants getting wrapped up in the aluminum foil of iniquity, believing every fly-by-night-prophet that tickles the ear but does not trouble the spirit. Will you please listen to Me? Avoid the false teachers and fruitless preachers. They praise Me with their lips, but their hearts are far from Me. They act like they love Me, but to love Me, you've got to do more than draw a heart on a piece a paper. You've got to serve Me. Hey. I served you, and I want nothing more than to be one with you. Sigh. They will be embarrassed to discover that their name was never written in the Book of Life (Revelation 20:15).[38] But I must speak truth because I am Truth. Look out for My signature.

Love,
　　　Author.

Think about how it feels to be falsely accused. If we don't like to be blamed for things we did not do, then why is it so shocking to imagine Christ saying, "Depart from me. I never knew you?" If we didn't sign something, we say immediately: "I never signed that. Don't affiliate me with him or her because if you do, I will be in debt paying for something I never approved. I will be in jail serving a sentence I never wrote." Now imagine Jesus. He took on sin debt that He never charged on His life account. He served a death sentence for a crime He didn't commit. And still, there are some among us who abuse Christ's love, distort the message, and pretend to represent him. Jesus says, "they honour me with their lips, but their heart is far from me" (Matthew 15:8).[39] Timothy says they have a form of godliness but deny the power thereof (2 Timothy 3:5).[40] This shouldn't be strange to us. If people can photocopy entire books without receiving permission from the author, then it is very likely that many people who say "Lord Lord," have also not received permission from the Author to do so.

It is so important to look out for God's signature. A signature, to me, is weightier than a name. Think about it. Anyone can say, "Shaun signed this," but my handwriting will never lie. In the same way, Jesus has a distinct signature. No one can sign it quite like He can. So, search for the signature. Don't just listen for the name.

WHAT JESUS MEANS WHEN HE SAYS "I NEVER KNEW YOU"

Matthew 7:23...And then will I profess unto them, **I never knew you**: depart from me, ye that work iniquity.

"I never knew you" does not mean I never saw you. God definitely sees. His eyes are in every place (Proverbs 15:3).[41] God sees the amount of human works we do. They are written on the front of the check. He sees the amount of people we lay hands on, He sees the demons we cast out, and He's heard about our great and mighty works. All of that is written on the front of the check. But, when He turns the check around, and there is no signature on the back, it is as if He never knew us. All that we have done for God is null and void because it was never reconciled in heaven's checkbook.

This teaches me not to get caught up in the business of making my name great before people so that God can hear about me. God hears with a different set of ears. God sees in secret. God loves a good "secret" (Psalm 91:1)![42] According to Matthew 7, God isn't moved by the senses the way we are. He made us with emotions, yes, and God moves in and through our ability to see, hear, feel, touch and taste. However, He's much more concerned about the deeper parts of our human composition. God is interested in the heart, mind, and soul of a man (Matthew 22:37).[43] He's not really into the church fabrications like we are. He's much more attracted to the beauty of holiness, the sanctity of true covenant, and the cries of a true worshipper than He is our cute rhythmic Rockette dances or our fancy little choir robes. He wants to know creation, and He wants to be known by creation. So the real question is, above what someone saw you do in church or what someone heard you say about God, "Do you know God and does God know you?

DO YOU KNOW GOD AND DOES GOD KNOW YOU?

Proverbs 8:17 I love them that love me;…

John 4:23 …for the Father seeketh such to worship Him.

I want to share a small sidebar story to clarify my point. Isn't it the funniest thing when that old high school enemy comes back in your life now that you are successful and important? She shows up to your book signing to get a picture with the now internationally recognized author, and you pass her by without taking a second glance. You, the author, have no clue who this lady is. To you, she's a bystander. To her, y'all are best buddies. But truthfully, the old high school friend has only reintroduced herself to you because of your success, not because you two have an authentic relationship. You see her. You just don't *know* her. You may have gone to school together, but you're not friends with her. Her picture is in the yearbook, but her number is not in your phonebook. Don't you see my point here? Jesus only knows and recognizes those who are not just crowd fillers, but friends. God is not looking for a fan club. God is looking for friendship. He wants to know and be known by those who love Him back. The emphasis is on the word "know." The Greek word for "know" in Matthew 7:23 is *ginōskō*. It is used as a Jewish idiom for intercourse. In other words, to know God and to be known by God is code language for intimacy.

The way Adam knew Eve (Genesis 4:1),[44] God wants to know His creation intimately. The way a husband should love his wife in the natural, Jesus wants to be loved in the supernatural by those who call him "Lord." To call some stranger "Lord" without having ever been intimate is almost as offensive as your biological child calling another random person "Mommy."

When Jesus says, "I never knew you," it doesn't mean He didn't create you, but it could mean He didn't procreate with you (spiritually speaking). He created me but He was never intimate with me. God and me never had true relationship. Him and I never conceived anything new. Yes. I, Shaun Saunders, went to church. But it wasn't until the church became more than a thing to do on Sunday, and it wasn't until I

Prayer: Lord, you are my inspiration. You are my motivation. You're the only reason I wake up. The rugged cross I will take it up. You're the producer of my production. One day you made me new. You're the conceiver of my conception. With one scent of your fruit my taste buds grew. I love you so much. Help me to know you more and to study you closely; to have you and to hold you. This is my desire.

treated my body as God's temple (1 Corinthians 3:16- 17)[45] that God and I began to court. We were enemies at one point in time, but now I am His bride. I belong to Him, and we belong together. I serve Him like a wife serves her husband and like a husband serves his wife. His every waking desire, I long to fulfill. His every tear, I yearn to wipe away. When He wakes me up at 5 AM and just wants to chitchat, I don't turn over and go to sleep. Instead, I sit up and listen. When He needs my time, my energy, and my body to edify His church, I do it freely and without reservation. As imperfect as I am, He still calls me His own. I am God's temple. He lives in me. Therefore, it is my responsibility to give myself to Him, seeking nothing in return for my labor.

This is what it means to know God, to be in love with God, and to serve God wholeheartedly—not for the preacher's offering or for worldly acclaim, but because God is the lover of your soul.

EVERYONE WILL GO TO HEAVEN, BUT FEW WILL STAY

Romans 14:10...For we shall all stand before the judgment seat of Christ.

I once heard a preacher say, "Everyone will go to heaven, but only a few will stay." I really don't know how true this statement is—I've never been to heaven–but if we consider the above Scripture, this may very well be the case. We will all stand before the judgment seat of Christ. That much is clear. What is unclear is if we will all sit at the Marriage Supper of the Lamb (Revelation 19:9).[46] I can't speak for you, but I want to go to heaven and stay there. I want to stand there, I want to sit there, I want to sing there and I want to snore there (well, I probably won't snore but if snoring happens there, I want to do it!) I don't want to hear God say, "Depart from me." But honestly speaking, neither does God. God doesn't take pleasure in saying, "Depart from me" because God is not willing that any man perish (2 Peter 3:9).[47] I believe God will be in more of a dilemma than we will ever be on judgment day. God would love to endorse everything that His creation has done, but according to the Word of God, He can't. God will not compromise His Word for anyone (Malachi 3:6)[48] and God can't sign off on anything that does not resemble Himself. If you don't know Christ yet, how about you make this easier on both parties? Get to know Jesus intimately before the clock strikes judgment day.

DON'T JUDGE THE INK BY ITS COLOR

2 Timothy 2:19 …the Lord knoweth them that are his.

When we all get to heaven, we will be shocked to discover that some of the pens we threw away, thinking they were dry and unusable, are the ones offering us a seat at the table. Meanwhile, the people we thought were so usable will be a part of the "many" unfortunate souls to whom the Lord will say, "depart from me." Before I end this chronicle, I want to remind you of 2 Timothy 2:19: "The Lord knoweth them that are His." The key is the Lord, not us. Not one human being knows who will make it in and who will not. So, do as Paul would do: study to be quiet, mind your own business, and do your own work with your own hands (1 Thessalonians 4:11).[49] The Lord knoweth them that are His. Let's be careful never to judge anyone (Matthew 7:1).[50] We can become so distracted by the color of a pen that we totally forget to see if the ink is actually working. Don't judge the ink by its color, the denomination by its doctrine, or the atheist by his confession. Just don't judge! None of us has a monopoly on heaven, so you are wasting your time handpicking the faithful apart from the fakeful. That's not your job. Only God knows. Don't walk around with your nose up, sniffing people and looking for a long white dress or a black suit to authenticate someone's relationship with God. Focus on loving God and loving others. If you love God the right way, you won't even have time to judge anybody else.

ABANDONING THE WILL OF THE CHILD

Matthew 7:21-23 Not every one that saith unto me, Lord, Lord, shall enter into the kingdom of heaven; but **he that doeth the will of my Father** which is in heaven.

In order to do the will of the Father, we must first abandon the will of the child. God's promises are available to everyone, but don't get it twisted, God is not the author of every manuscript submitted to Heaven's publishing house. He doesn't author confusion (1 Corinthians 14:33),[51] He can't publish forgery, and He certainly won't endorse sin. You can scream, "Lord, Lord" as loud as you want, but God cannot author your life until you've given Him the pen. The only way we can enter into the kingdom, according to Matthew 7:21, is if we depart from our will and do the Father's will. We've got to file bankruptcy on our egocentric desires, and enlist in God's army and obey His commands. If we don't, then God won't endorse the back of our checks. Why? Because He knows we are a bounced check waiting to happen. But the moment we confess Christ as Lord and Savior, He opens up a new account on our behalf, and God's promises are available to us. The closer we get to God, the farther we get from ourselves. We begin to embrace the new creature that God is forming within us, and not before long, we find ourselves sharing the good news with someone else. These are all attributes of the Father's will: exemplifying Christ's love, standing on God's Word, sharing the Good News with others, resisting evil at all costs (for the sake of Christ and church), and looking unto Jesus, the Author and Finisher of our faith.

I encourage you, readers, to emulate Christ in all things, for God's reputation hinges on our ability to represent Him rightly. Don't ruin His signature. Don't be content with being unusable. God wants to use you to do great things for His kingdom. God doesn't only want the credit after you've won a Grammy, scored a touchdown, or lied about the deceased at his or her funeral; God wants to author your entire life.

So what are you waiting for? Just hand over your horrible, illegible handwriting, and allow God's signature to become your new, permanent "John Hancock." Give God your disposable pen so He can author your faith, guide your finish, and usher you from the joy of abundant life into the ecstasy of eternal life.

See you in heaven!

Question for Introspection
ᑐ_____ᕲ

------------◈------------
Lord: Like Adam knew Eve, I want to know You. Like David tended sheep, I want to study You. You are the mastermind behind the mirror and through Your reflection I see myself clearer. So what can I do to make You smile? What can I say to make You blush? In the silence of the wind...that's where I feel Your touch. In the echo of the storm, I sense Your rain of peace. Many people want a rush, but I want to reside with You. Author, I give You the pen. Finisher, I give You my heart. Father, I ask You to guide my feet. I yearn to do Your will even if I never get the mansion on top of the hill. Sign my life, Lord. You can have all of me. Amen
------------◈------------

1) Does the Lord know you? If so, how do you know?

Practical Points

1

You can hang around the Christian crowd and scream "Lord, Lord" every Sunday, but if God doesn't have a relational memory of you, your cries are on mute. He does not know you. If God says, "I never knew you," what He's really saying, in essence is, "I can't recognize my signature in your life. I can't see a reflection of myself in you." Therefore, those who don't reflect God and those who haven't departed from sin, must depart from God. Heaven has no angelic understudies.

2

Examine your life and evaluate, most specifically, those areas you think are God-led and at the same time self-gratifying. Think twice before you sign your life to someone whom God has not preauthorized. When in doubt, ask God for scriptural confirmation (James 1:5).[52] If you're still unsure, just be still (Psalms 46:10).[53] I would hate for you to forge God's signature on a check that He would never endorse.

3

Popular preachers and big congregations don't always indicate God's endorsement. God signs the back of our checks once the front of it reads "all about you, Jesus." Numbers don't name God. Power does. "For the kingdom of God is not in word, but in power" (1 Corinthians 4:20).[54] God's power, God's seal, and God's Spirit are divine signatures that cannot be forged. The power belongs to God (Psalms 62:11),[55] the seal is established by God (2 Corinthians 1:21-22),[56] and the spirit of God transforms (2 Corinthians 3:17-18).[57] If you're ever visiting a church and there is no evidence of transformation, exit as soon as possible.

4

When your ink stops working, there is another pen in someone else's hand willing to do what you refuse to do. But be aware, the blessing God had prepared for you, and the check that had your name on it, will be given to another better than you (1 Samuel 15:28).[58] Why? Because no one is indispensable. This is Scriptural. David was the pen that replaced Saul (2 Samuel 5:3),[59] Matthias was the pen that replaced Judas (Acts 1:25-26),[58] and Christ was the pen that replaced Adam (Romans 5:19).[61]

5

It was Jesus, the ultimate pen Refiller, who died on the cross to restore sinful humanity into right standing with God. In order to reign with Him, you are going to suffer with Him (2 Timothy 2:12).[62] But be of good cheer. A true follower of Jesus cannot bypass the trail that leads to the cross. Eventually, something in you must die out of you so that Christ can restore you without you.

Scripture Glossary

ଔ_____ୠ

[1]**John 9:11** *He answered and said, A man that is called Jesus made clay, and anointed mine eyes, and said unto me, Go to the pool of Siloam, and wash: and I went and washed, and I received sight.*

[2]**Hebrews 5:9** *And being made perfect, he became the author of eternal salvation unto all them that obey him.*

[3]**1 Corinthians 1:25** *Because the foolishness of God is wiser than men; and the weakness of God is stronger than men.*

[4]**Proverbs 25:28** *He that hath no rule over his own spirit is like a city that is broken down, and without walls.*

[5]**John 14:6** *Jesus saith unto him, I am the way, the truth, and the life: no man cometh unto the Father, but by me.*

[6]**Luke 12:7** *But even the very hairs of your head are all numbered. Fear not therefore: ye are of more value than many sparrows.*

[7]**John 14:26** *But the Comforter, which is the Holy Ghost, whom the Father will send in my name, he shall teach you all things, and bring all things to your remembrance, whatsoever I have said unto you.*

[8]**Romans 3:23** *For all have sinned, and come short of the glory of God.*

[9]**1 Peter 4:18** *And if the righteous scarcely be saved, where shall the ungodly and the sinner appear?*

[10]**James 4:14** *Whereas ye know not what shall be on the morrow. For what is your life? It is even a vapour, that appeareth for a little time, and then vanisheth away.*

[11]**Psalm 46:1** *God is our refuge and strength, a very present help in trouble.*

[12]**John 4:34** *Jesus saith unto them, My meat is to do the will of him that sent me, and to finish his work.*

[13]**Luke 14:30** *Saying, This man began to build, and was not able to finish.*

[14]**Philippians 1:6** *Being confident of this very thing, that he which hath begun a good work in you will perform it until the day of Jesus Christ.*

[15]**John 10:10** *The thief cometh not, but for to steal, and to kill, and to destroy: I am come that they might have life, and that they might have it more abundantly.*

[16]**Romans 6:23** *For the wages of sin is death; but the gift of God is eternal life through Jesus Christ our Lord.*

[17]**James 1:15** *Then when lust hath conceived, it bringeth forth sin:*

and sin, when it is finished, bringeth forth death.

[18]**Proverbs 6:16-19** *These six things doth the LORD hate: yea, seven are an abomination unto him: A proud look, a lying tongue, and hands that shed innocent blood, An heart that deviseth wicked imaginations, feet that be swift in running to mischief, A false witness that speaketh lies, and he that soweth discord among brethren.*

[19]**Romans 8:2** *For the law of the Spirit of life in Christ Jesus hath made me free from the law of sin and death.*

[20]**Deuteronomy 1:2** *(There are eleven days' journey from Horeb by the way of mount Seir unto Kadeshbarnea.)*

[21]**Romans 6:17-18** *But God be thanked, that ye were the servants of sin, but ye have obeyed from the heart that form of doctrine which was delivered you. Being then made free from sin, ye became the servants of righteousness.*

[22]**James 4:7** *Submit yourselves therefore to God. Resist the devil, and he will flee from you.*

[23]**2 Corinthians 4:4** *In whom the god of this world hath blinded the minds of them which believe not, lest the light of the glorious gospel of Christ, who is the image of God, should shine unto them.*

[24]**Acts 9:3-5** *And as he journeyed, he came near Damascus: and suddenly there shined round about him a light from heaven: And he fell to the earth, and heard a voice saying unto him, Saul, Saul, why persecutest thou me? And he said, Who art thou, Lord? And the Lord said, I am Jesus whom thou persecutest: it is hard for thee to kick against the pricks.*

[25]**John 16:13** *Howbeit when he, the Spirit of truth, is come, he will guide you into all truth: for he shall not speak of himself; but whatsoever he shall hear, that shall he speak: and he will shew you things to come.*

[26]**Matthew 7:13-14** *Enter ye in at the strait gate: for wide is the gate, and broad is the way, that leadeth to destruction, and many there be which go in thereat: Because strait is the gate, and narrow is the way, which leadeth unto life, and few there be that find it.*

[27]**Hebrews 12:1** *Wherefore seeing we also are compassed about with so great a cloud of witnesses, let us lay aside every weight, and the sin which doth so easily beset us, and let us run with patience the race that is set before us.*

[28]**2 Timothy 4:7** *I have fought a good fight, I have finished my course, I have kept the faith.*

[29]**Acts 2:39** *For the promise is unto you, and to your children, and to all that are afar off, even as many as the LORD our God shall call.*

[30]**Hebrews 9:15** *And for this cause he is the mediator of the new testament, that by means of death, for the redemption of the transgressions that were under the first testament, they which are called might receive the promise of eternal inheritance.*

[31]**Ephesians 6:13** *Wherefore take unto you the whole armour of God, that ye may be able to withstand in the evil day, and having done all, to stand.*

[32]**2 Corinthians 5:17** *Therefore if any man be in Christ, he is a new creature: old things are passed away; behold, all things are become new.*

[33]**Proverbs 24:16** *for a just man falleth seven times, and riseth up again: but the wicked shall fall into mischief.*

[34]**Philippians 3:14** *I press toward the mark for the prize of the high calling of God in Christ Jesus.*

[35]**Psalm 121:1** *I will lift up mine eyes unto the hills, from whence cometh my help.*

[36]**Isaiah 9:6** *For unto us a child is born, unto us a son is given: and the government shall be upon his shoulder: and his name shall be called Wonderful, Counsellor, The mighty God, The everlasting Father, The Prince of Peace.*

[37]**Matthew 7:15** *Beware of fale prophets, which come to you in sheep's clothing, but inwardly they are ravening wolves.*

[38]**Revelation 20:15** *And whosoever was not found written in the book of life was cast into the lake of fire.*

[39]**Matthew 15:8** *This people draweth nigh unto me with their mouth, and honoureth me with their lips; but their heart is far from me.*

[40]**2 Timothy 3:5** *Having a form of godliness, but denying the power thereof: from such turn away.*

[41]**Proverbs 15:3** *The eyes of the LORD are in every place, beholding the evil and the good.*

[42]**Psalm 91:1** *He that dwelleth in the secret place of the most High shall abide under the shadow of the Almighty.*

[43]**Matthew 22:37** *Jesus said unto him, Thou shalt love the Lord thy God with all thy heart, and with all thy soul, and with all thy mind.*

[44]**Genesis 4:1** *And Adam knew Eve his wife; and she conceived, and bare Cain, and said, I have gotten a man from the LORD.*

[45]**1 Corinthians 3:16-17** *Know ye not that ye are the temple of God, and that the Spirit of God dwelleth in you? If any man defile the temple of God, him shall God destroy; for the temple of God is holy, which temple ye are.*

[46]**Revelation 19:9** *And he saith unto me, Write, Blessed are they which are called unto the marriage supper of the Lamb. And he*

saith unto me, These are the true sayings of God.

[47]**2 Peter 3:9** *The Lord is not slack concerning his promise, as some men count slackness; but is longsuffering to us-ward, not willing that any should perish, but that all should come to repentance.*

[48]**Malachi 3:6** *For I am the LORD, I change not; therefore ye sons of Jacob are not consumed.*

[49]**1 Thessalonians 4:11** *And that ye study to be quiet, and to do your own business, and to work with your own hands, as we commanded you.*

[50]**Matthew 7:1** *Judge not, that ye be not judged.*

[51]**1 Corinthians 14:33** *For God is not the author of confusion, but of peace, as in all churches of the saints.*

[52]**James 1:5** *If any of you lack wisdom, let him ask of God, that giveth to all men liberally, and upbraideth not; and it shall be given him.*

[53]**Psalm 46:10** *Be still, and know that I am God: I will be exalted among the heathen, I will be exalted in the earth.*

[54]**1 Corinthians 4:20** *For the kingdom of God is not in word, but in power.*

[55]**Psalm 62:11** *God hath spoken once; twice have I heard this; that power belongeth unto God.*

[56]**2 Corinthians 1:21-22** *Now he which stablisheth us with you in Christ, and hath anointed us, is God; Who hath also sealed us, and given the earnest of the Spirit in our hearts.*

[57]**2 Corinthians 3:17-18** *Now the Lord is that Spirit: and where the Spirit of the Lord is, there is liberty. But we all, with open face*

beholding as in a glass the glory of the Lord, are changed into the same image from glory to glory, even as by the Spirit of the Lord.

[58]**1 Samuel 15:28** *And Samuel said unto him, The LORD hath rent the kingdom of Israel from thee this day, and hath given it to a neighbour of thine, that is better than thou.*

[59]**2 Samuel 5:3** *So all the elders of Israel came to the king to Hebron; and king David made a league with them in Hebron before the LORD: and they anointed David king over Israel.*

[60]**Acts 1:25-26** *That he may take part of this ministry and apostleship, from which Judas by transgression fell, that he might go to his own place. And they gave forth their lots; and the lot fell upon Matthias; and he was numbered with the eleven apostles.*

[61]**Romans 5:19** *For as by one man's disobedience many were made sinners, so by the obedience of one shall many be made righteous.*

[62]**2 Timothy 2:12** *If we suffer, we shall also reign with him: if we deny him, he also will deny us.*

OPENING A GATE

Are we Locked in God or Just Looped Around?

∘_____∘

*Therefore my beloved brethren, be ye stedfast, **unmoveable**, always abounding in the work of the Lord...*
1 Corinthians 15:58

*M*y home church is located in north Newark, New Jersey, where gang violence, drug dealings, broken homes, and hideaway criminals exist. *Wisdom is indeed the principal thing.* So, the church has invested in a home security system for the inside, and erected a chain link fence for the outside. There is a 12-foot high charcoal fence around the perimeter of the church grounds, separating the church property from the neighborhood sidewalk. That's what you see when you approach the one and only Holiness Pentecostal Church of Christ. Yup, a high gate that looks a bit scary and uninviting, but a gate with purpose—to discourage trespassers from the outside and to protect the people and property on the inside.

This morning, I deactivated the alarm and headed outside to open the gate for 5 a.m. prayer. I noticed something peculiar. The chain and lock were choked tightly around the opening sections of the gate and the lock was fastened firmly around the chain. *Uh oh.* I had no key for the lock. *How would I open the gate without a key? Who locked this gate anyway? We haven't used this lock in years!* I got angry at first; but then, when I realized I couldn't do anything about it, I calmed myself down and proceeded to walk toward the gate. The closer I got to touching the gate, the more obvious it became to me that it wasn't really locked. It was just looped. The chain and lock were looped around the opening parts of the gate to trick trespassers into believing it was locked, but it also allowed easy access for those coming to Morning Prayer. *Ah,*

I see said the blind man. If I were close enough to the gate, I could see the truth and gain entry without a key. But, if I were far enough away from the gate, I believed a lie and would've been tricked into turning around. *Brilliant.* So what I thought was locked was, in fact, looped. I saw God in this and asked myself, "Am I locked in God or am I just looped around?"

AM I LOCKED IN GOD OR JUST LOOPED AROUND?

As soon as I finished praying, I ran upstairs to look up the definition for lock and the definition for loop. I knew I had heard God this morning and I was excited to write a chronicle about this encounter! I never imagined what I would find after looking up these simple words. First, I discovered six definitions for lock. Then, I discovered three definitions for loop! God used every definition to speak volumes of revelation to me. *Sometimes the best heavenly revelation is hidden in mundane objects and secular resources.* Let me share with you how God expanded my knowledge of Him by seeing Him in simple definitions.

According to Merriam-Webster, "looped ribbons serve as perfect *ornament.*" The definition continues: "When something is looped, like a shoelace for example, it is not tight and "*forms* a partly open curve through which *another* line can be passed."[i] Wow! Three simple words jumped out at me, describing perfectly what it meant to be looped in God: one was *form*, the other was *another*, and the last was *ornament*.

DEFINITION #1:
HOW GOD USED "FORM" TO SPEAK TO ME.

In Merriam's world, the word "form" was written to mean "shape" or to be shaped by, but the Spirit brought 2 Timothy 3:5 to my mind. Here is what it says:

---

i "loop." <u>Merriam-Webster Online Dictionary</u>. 2008. Merriam-Webster Online. 7 May 2008 <u>http://www.merriam-webster.com/dictionary/loop</u>

2 Timothy 3:5 Having a form of godliness, but denying the power thereof; from such turn away.

What does "form of godliness" mean exactly? Well, in this context, a *form* is an illusion. A form is a false perception. Those who have a form of godliness pretend to put on the whole armor of God (Ephesians 6:11),[1] but never get dressed for battle. They imitate, perform, and mimic those who fight, but if caught by themselves, they are powerless and unreliable. *Now let's be honest.* We have all "formed" at one point in our lives—telling jokes we didn't mean, laughing at jokes that weren't funny, performing roles in school plays, pretending to enjoy a movie, a job, or a person we actually despised—so we know firsthand how this goes. Mere performers have great stage presence, but no power. They put on a magnificent show, but they lack substance and truth. Similarly, people who have a form of godliness know how to per-*form.* Let me dig a bit deeper.

I recently read an article in the Stanford Daily about an imposter student. The student wanted to attend this prestigious school so badly that she, "...spent eight months posing as a biology major, buying textbooks, attending classes, and cramming with friends for exams she couldn't take." [ii] She never enrolled. She didn't have an email account. She certainly couldn't graduate, and she crawled in through the cracks of windows every night because she didn't have access into the dorm. Yet, she attended class faithfully and wore the college memorabilia *as if she were* a matriculating student.

This gets to the heart of what "form of godliness" means: *as if you were.* To have a form of godliness is to act as if you were a student of Christ, but in reality, you are not. You talk the talk, but you do not walk the walk. Like the imposter student, you show up to church and wear the appropriate uniform, but at the end of the day, you are like the actor on the stage—great show, no substance. You are looped and not locked. You walk with the crowd but you

---

ii Wasley, Paula. "For Impostor Student at Stanford, Cardinal Rule Was Just Showing Up." The Chronicle of Higher Education (2007)

are not a follower of Christ.

How do we avoid these loopers? Well, apostle Paul tells Timothy to leave the pretenders alone. In fact, his last four words in 2 Timothy 3:5 are straightforward instructions for how to avoid those who have a form of godliness: "from such turn away." The same message rings true for us as well. We've got to learn how to turn away from performers. If we don't, we'll eventually turn into one.

------------◇------------

The church has more imposter Christians than learning institutions have imposter students. This Stanford story made headlines once or twice, but this fraudulent stuff happens, unnoticed, in church every Sunday. Are you "forming" or being formed? Are you projecting or being perfected?

------------◇------------

DEFINITION #2:
HOW GOD USED "ANOTHER" TO SPEAK TO ME

Looped Christians always have *another* reason not to come to church, another wrinkly issue up their sleeve, another god that gets in the way of serving Jesus. Another hole, another role, another excuse to Loopty Loo. You can tell a looped perpetrator not by the books he carries to Stanford, but by the windows he cracks open for *another* imposter to enter into. In other words, looped Christians flock together, and they are really cunning and crafty for a while. But after three months, they hate each other. They fight over unnecessary things, they are addicted to drama, and they are easily jealous of *another* close friend if he or she gets too close to you. Territorial. That's the word. These kinds of Christians are territorial, petty and immature. If you ask them for a favor, they will throw their good deeds in your face until you do *another* favor for them.

What else? Oh, they justify, justify, justify and they think it's O.K. to interweave the lines of their past into the holy lesson plans of their future. Another line to pass through and they must "have their cake and eat it too." They like to mix clean and unclean, holy and unholy, and they often mingle with confused and unstable people so that they can feel normal about their dysfunction (James 1:8).[2] They joke around way too much and criticize everyone who has a sincere heart toward God. And they love to give excuses! Excuse after excuse, a looped person will present the best case for sinful misconduct and, if you're not careful, will convince you to alter your conviction in order to accommodate their unrepentant life-decisions.

DEFINITION #3:
ORNAMENTS GLISTEN FOR A FEW MONTHS

Ornaments are only good for a season. Anyone will tell you that. And winter is the best time to purchase the greatest ornaments (since Kwanzaa, Hanukkah, and Christmas all take place during the winter season). Well, here's the thing about ornamentally looped Christians. The same way no one sees the Christmas glistening glass balls or those flaming menorah candles in the summer, ornament-like churchgoers are seen for a limited time. Ornamental loopers. We all know a few. They clock in and they clock out. They commit to a specific task today and before you look up, they're filing for ecclesial unemployment tomorrow. Most times, they try to steal all of the attention away from everyone else while they are there in attendance for five Sundays out of the year. Churchgoers beware! Ornamental Christians are said to swing from trees and doorknobs and are very likely to fall down and break easily.

Form, another, ornament. Here's how they all come together. When a Christian becomes overly concerned with "(per)forming" a role as a temporary "ornament," there will always be an opening through which "another" line has permission to pass. *Always.* So, instead of allowing space for *another*, why don't we focus more on being God's significant other? Why don't we remind ourselves that we are the Bride of Christ and joint heirs to the throne? We should be happy to embrace all that God has for us, instead of *forming* and *performing* a role. We should be excited about living a life that is faithful to the call and commission of God, instead of being a temporary ornament. We should aspire to be God's instrument, not the church's ornament; for if I am God's instrument, then God can play through me whenever God chooses and God can use me however God wills.

DEFINITION #4:
THE SNOBBY LOOPER

On the other side of this loop spectrum is another kind of Christian, however. Those whose struggles are so deeply hidden from the surface that they pretend to be perfect in all things and end up becoming effective in no thing; those who work overtime to portray an image of godliness to the point that they will dismiss you from their presence if you damage their reputation. I bet you know some of these folks as well. Looped Christians on this side of the spectrum think it is perfectly O.K. to judge others (Matthew 7:1)[3] and we use our own experiential authority and skewed opinion to condemn you, the sinner, to hell. We never wash clothes because, let's face it, our clothes never smell. We never clean dishes in the church because that's not a part of our job description. We are called to the nations, not the sink.

Saints, Beware! Both the high-minded Christian and the half-hearted Christian are not only loopy and unpredictable, but they are dangerous to hang around for extended periods of time. How do I know? Well here's the truth. I've had to repent for being both a self-righteous looper and a justify, justify, justify looper. I've drank from two different cups (1 Corinthians 10:21)[4] and I've attended two different parties. I used to pretend my life was perfect at times, and at other times, when no one was looking, I searched Scriptures to find an excuse to do what I knew was wrong. That's why I fight every day to be locked in God. I fight everyday against the temptation of self-righteous arrogance on the one hand, and the temptation to justify what my flesh craves to do under the guise of spiritless reasoning on the other. That's why I need Christ just like you.

So if any of the above descriptions fit your spiritual outfit, let me tell you the truth in love. You are looped and not locked. But, don't feel bad. At least you're on the gate.

DEFINITION #5:
LAZY, LOOPY, & DISTRACTED PREACHERS

In the music industry, a loop is used to describe a series of repeated instructions until a terminating condition is reached. When a song, for instance, is on loop, it repeats until the person in control of the music device tells it to stop. *Beware of the tendency to loop your radio on the song titled "Distraction." Distractions will always cause you to repeat (loop) things unnecessarily.* But when I saw this definition, I thought to myself, "this is a perfect way to articulate my concerns about the looped Christian leaders in the pulpit." I've often wondered, "How many sermons are on loop and how many souls are lost as a result of it?" There are so many so-called teachers of the gospel who learn, learn, learn, or should I say, loop, loop, loop, but never access the knowledge of the truth (2 Timothy 3:7)[5], leaving whole households susceptible to subversion because the message they hear on Sunday is either stale, borrowed, or stolen from the internet. Now, it's one thing for the Lord to tell you to preach the same message for 50 days. But, it's another thing altogether when you have no fresh Word from God because you haven't been to the holy fountain. Let me dig deeper.

To read what Dr. Martin Luther King, Jr. says about Jesus is nice. To hear what Pastor Sheryl Brady says about Jesus is cute. But who do *you* say Jesus is? This is the selfsame question Jesus asked the disciples (Matthew 16:15)[6] and this is the question that every preacher must ask himself or herself regularly.

Believe it or not, many, many preachers are churchy by nature, and have learned the art of preaching through osmosis, not desire. They had to watch the painter paint every Sunday morning whether they liked the color mixtures or not, whether the wall needed a new coat or not, whether the painter was even good or not. Church to them was nothing more than a chore from childbirth that they just couldn't get out of. So now, we have pastors of every sort who can mimic their preaching predecessors, loop around the church, holler and hoop and yet, they still don't know who Jesus is.

How do I know if I'm forming or not?

Sometimes, the only way to figure out if you actually know God or not, you've got to step out of the loop of preaching circles and love on God in private. Examine yourself and pay attention to the way you react to God in private quarters. If you notice that you and God are strangers in secret, then you're probably putting on a show in public. Simple as that. If you and God have nothing to talk about unless there is a microphone system with exceptional sound quality and an audience of onlookers to cheer you on, then you and God are not in covenant. At best, you are distant lovers. At worse, you are complete strangers.

Sometimes you've got to leave the commentaries alone and commit to a consecrated prayer time. Sometimes you've got to open the Bible for yourself, and not just to get a spicy word for an unseasoned people. Who died and made you head chef anyway? The word of God is delivered, not concocted. The people of God are His sheep, not your homemade litmus test. If we do not get delivered from the loopy mentality, the people will ask for a rhema word and will, instead, receive a recycled one.[iii]

Which brings me to another sidebar point. When a preacher becomes too tired or distracted to seek God's face and wait for an answer, she needs a vacation, not another preaching engagement. Preachers can burn out very easily and many of them don't know how to say, "Not today. I need time with God." But preachers, your spiritual life is at stake. You've got to learn how to

---

[iii]*Rhema* is a Greek word that means "the spoken word;" Romans 10:8; Matthew 4:4[7-8]

say "no" sometimes. I know you have a hefty itinerary, but if the itinerary inhibits personal consecration time, then your lack of study and worship will infect the learning environment (church). You will cause God's people to loop, and it will be your fault.

Please hear me out.

Learn how to rest in the presence of God before you fall asleep behind the pulpit wheel. The pulpit is not a platform where I, the preacher, get to ingest my spiritual steroid for the week. It is not the place where I get to excite the masses for ego relief or as a means to redirect my depression through catharsis. Too many hungry sheep depend on a shepherd apt to teach and ready to supply God's people with fresh heavenly food, not stale leftovers. Imagine how poisoned the Israelites would have become if God fed them expired manna (Exodus 16:19-21).[9]

Definition #6:
You're Out of the Loop

The sixth way we use the word "loop" is to exclude one group and include another. Usually, we notice this when people say things like, "I'm in the loop," or "she's out of the loop;" and what that usually implies is that I am special and she is not. Well, this prompted me to think about some of the Christian superstars of our day, be they denominational celebrities or renowned recording artists. If we are honest, some of the most conceited Christians are popular singers and preachers. So, I asked myself, "Shaun, if God makes your name great in the earth, will you self-glory because you've been accepted into the Christian VIP section of the sold-out concert?" *But I didn't stop there.* I also thought, "Shaun, are you only in the Christian loop when you're around people that serve the Lord, but when you are away from the church parking lot, the world sees another you?" I waited. I thought about it. And then I answered my own self-examination questions. I would advise you to do the same. If you don't, you risk becoming a loopy, cocky, exclusivist and money-hungry Christian, especially toward your unsaved family members.

The unsaved "out of the loop" thing is really big nowadays, and all of us are guilty of doing it. We receive the gift of salvation and now we are technically "in the salvation loop." But the gift of salvation does not give us the right to be condescending. The Bible instructs us to, "Do good unto all men, especially unto them who are of the household of faith" (Galatians 6:10).[10] All means all. Our unsaved family and friends should never get the impression that we are better than they are because we "know" God and they do not. We should never give off a "holier than thou" vibe, especially when we aren't living as holy as we pretend to be.

Let's be mindful of the weight of our words and deeds. Let's love one another and encourage everyone. We may never realize it now, but what we say (or do not say) could have an eternal impact on the lives of everyone around us. It is our duty as Christians to walk in the light of Christ with the hopes that, one day, all will be in the loop of salvation.

3 LOCK DEFINITIONS: SEATBELT, HAIR, AND WRESTLING

Now here is the opposite of loop:

Definition #1: To be locked in God is to be uncomfortably fastened like a seatbelt in the protection of God's care. When you are locked in God, you are airtight. You are so tightly knit to God that even when you want to run away, you can't get farther than the door. If you are locked in God and the pastor says something you don't agree with, your relationship with God supersedes your companionship with your pastor, and you'll find yourself in prayer again, singing in the choir again, or greeting visitors as if you had never considered leaving the church. You, my dear sister, are locked in God.

Definition #2: Locks are used (in ancient biblical history and at present) to describe the hair. Samson, a Nazarite in the Old Testament, lost supernatural strength because a looper distracted him. He was not as steadfast and unmovable as he appeared to be. He fell asleep in the lap of the tempter, and before he knew it, his locks were cut, and "she had called for a man, and caused him to shave off the seven locks of his head; began to afflict him, and his strength went from him" (Judges 16:19).[11] Delilah was a looper, and loopers love to attack locks! Just like those who "form another ornament," Delilah had two pairs of scissors in her back pocket and invited another looper in to finish Samson off. If you are locked in God, don't allow the looping bullies to cut off your strength. Disentangle yourself from these bad split ends and if need be, find a new beautician! You can't afford to go another day with damaged locks.

Pause. Many of us have lost strength because we found comfort in an accomplice's lap. I know he is nice, but if you knew he was an anointing killer, would you have fallen asleep at his house? If you knew she was a dream crusher, would you have agreed to a spring break trip with her? Too many Christian women confess to having had a one-life stand with the man who sleeps with her and causes her to fall, only to turn around and fall asleep after she's messed up. So, here you are—sitting in the bed, convicted, nauseous and trying to hold back tears. The guy who persuaded you to fall is snoring.   Or even worse, he leaves. *Unpause.*

Proverbs 4:16 For they sleep not except they have done mischief; and their sleep is taken away unless they cause some to fall.

Definition #3: Wrestlemania "Lock." As a former wrestling fanatic, the lock has another special meaning for me. In the league of professional wrestling, there is a maneuver called "The Lock." The lock is a holding position used to chokehold the opponent. Any competitor can perform this move, so the trick is to do it to your opponent before it gets done to you. Once the lock is applied onto the opponent, audiences know the match is over because the lock is a stronghold position most cannot escape. There are many layers of revelation in this analogy, but I'll just highlight one.

Once you get a hold of your opponent (be it a physical

addiction, an antagonizing memory, or an inner struggle), do not let go. Lock it up, and don't give the old man room to resurrect. You are too close to winning the tournament to let go of your locked position. Be steadfast, unmoveable, always abounding in the work of the Lord. I know you might empathize with your opponent but guilt, empathy, or trying to be there for her because she was there for you, are all tricks the opponent uses to convince us to loosen our locked position (1 Peter 5:8).[12] How many times have you loosened your grip and become captive to the very thing you once captured? If you loosen your grip, take it from me, your opponent will escape and will turn around and place you in the very chokehold out of which he or she escaped. Hold on. Tighten your grip. Mimic Jacob's "locked" position in Genesis 32:26.

Genesis 32:26 And he said, Let me go, for the day breaketh. And he said, I will not let thee go, except thou bless me.

Lord, I don't just want to be locked in you. I want to be Your lock. For if I am Your lock, then You can be my key. And if You are my key, then You can open me up when others need access to You and lock me down when it's time to protect that which I am withholding.

Decide today that you will not let this opponent go until you are declared the winner of the wrestling match. You are victorious over this (Romans 7:23, Romans 13:14)![13-14]

BECAUSE GOD EXPECTS HOLINESS

"Why fight to be steadfast and unmoveable? Why should I be locked in God? Is it really that serious whether I'm looped or locked? I just want to be in God--looped, locked, lazy or lame. As long as I'm in God, I'm good." Let me give you a four-word answer and an analogy to match: *Because God expects holiness.* Commit it to memory, stamp it on a T-shirt, write a chorus line if you must, but, however you do it, remember the Scripture: "Be ye holy, for I am holy" (1 Peter 1:16).[15] It can't get any simpler than that. God expects us to be holy, God desires that we exchange our fleshly wardrobe with the newness of life, which is created in righteousness and true holiness. (Ephesians 4:22-24),[16] and God is most pleased when we turn His commandment into an opportunity for communion. You can never be too locked in God. You can never become too "saved." The closer you get to God, the more God will shine through you.

Now, here's the closing analogy.

A middle-aged mother rushes out of the house and does not take the time to lock her child in a seatbelt. Instead, she loops the belt around just to make it appear to the cops (if she were pulled over) that she didn't deserve a ticket. They get into a car accident. The innocent child dies. The funeral is filled with sad songs and regret. Tragedies like this happen time and time again, but think about how many spiritual mothers have lost their children due to a looped seatbelt. The point is this: the lock is more important than the appearance thereof. Holiness is more important than happiness. Pleasing God is far greater than pleasing others. *Please hear me today.* God wants you to buckle up in Him. God wants to hold you tightly, love you closely, and share heaven's treasure chest with you ultimately. If you are not locked, then you are certainly not completely surrendered either. So, go ahead and surrender your all to Him. God loves you more than you could ever know.

Wherever you are, whoever you are, be sure that you are locked in God and not just looped around.

---------- ◈ ----------

Prayer: Lord, strip away any form of godliness in me. Help me not to allow another false god to distract me from You, the true and living God. I don't want to form another ornament. I want to be your permanent instrument.

---------- ◈ ----------

Questions for Introspection

CB_____&O

1) How many loopholes have you allowed to interfere with your Christian walk this year? (Exodus 20:3)[17]

2) Are you God's permanent instrument or are you the church's ornament? If you are somewhere in between, choose the instrument you will play or the box you will be stored in after Christmas. Decide and don the nametag you would like people to identify you by today (Joshua 24:15).[18]

Practical Points

CB_____&O

1   A true worshipper desires to be God's lock. If you would decide to lock yourself in God, then your permanent change will cause a domino effect. Soon, even your family will see how important it is for them to be locked in God, too.

2 Allow yourself to be locked in God like money inside a protected vault. The thief will not have access to steal anything from your beautiful fenced-in house if you are locked in God. Those songs about taking back what the devil stole will be null and void because the enemy won't have the access code into the treasures of your heart. There will be no space for another. No loopholes. No second best.

3   We wrestle and fight to be locked in God so that, in the end, we obtain a true balance, not a championship medal. We need balance to serve God and balance to reach people. A false balance is an abomination (Proverbs 11:1).[19] Be real at all times!

4 Preachers, don't loop! Sunday school teachers, don't loop! Ushers, don't loop! Believers, don't loop! The unchurched have a special way of discerning when your Christian walk is on loop and not LIVE! If you want to win souls for Christ, then be honest with yourself and recharge when necessary. Lock yourself in a private prayer closet with God and stay there until God gives you something fresh. And if you don't have a fresh Word for God's people, then give the pulpit, microphone, or bullhorn over to someone who does.

5 Ushers, gatekeepers, and greeters, hear me loud and clear. The next time someone walks up to the church doors, I dare you to greet them with these words: "You say you're a student of Christ, but show me your I.D." If they show you evidence of their matriculation (hopefully by inviting someone who is unchurched), let them through. If not, tell them to sneak through the window... just kidding!

Scripture Glossary

[1]**Ephesians 6:11** *Put on the whole armour of God, that ye may be able to stand against the wiles of the devil.*

[2]**James 1:8** *A double minded man is unstable in all his ways.*

[3]**Matthew 7:1** *Judge not, that ye be not judged.*

[4]**1 Corinthians 10:21** *Ye cannot drink the cup of the Lord, and the cup of devils: ye cannot be partakers of the Lord's table, and of the table of devils.*

[5]**2 Timothy 3:7** *Ever learning, and never able to come to the knowledge of the truth.*

6**Matthew 16:15** *He saith unto them, But whom say ye that I am?*

7**Romans 10:8** *But what saith it? The word is nigh thee, even in thy mouth, and in thy heart: that is, the word of faith, which we preach.*

8**Matthew 4:4** *But he answered and said, it is written, man shall not live by bread alone, but by every word that proceedeth out of the mouth of God.*

9**Exodus 16:19-21** *And Moses said, Let no man leave of it till the morning. Notwithstanding they hearkened not unto Moses; but some of them left of it until the morning, and it bred worms, and stank: and Moses was wroth with them. And they gathered it every morning, every man according to his eating: and when the sun waxed hot, it melted.*

10**Galatians 6:10** *As we have therefore opportunity, let us do good unto all men, especially unto them who are of the household of faith.*

11**Judges 16:19** *And she made him sleep upon her knees; and she called for a man, and she caused him to shave off the seven locks of his head; and she began to afflict him, and his strength went from him.*

12**1 Peter 5:8** *Be sober, be vigilant; because your adversary the devil, as a roaring lion, walketh about, seeking whom he may devour.*

13**Romans 7:23** *But I see another law in my members, warring against the law of my mind, and bringing me into captivity to the law of sin which is in my members.*

14**Romans 13:14** *But put ye on the Lord Jesus Christ, and make not provision for the flesh, to fulfil the lusts thereof.*

15**1 Peter 1:16** *Because it is written, Be ye holy; for I am holy.*

[16]**Ephesians 4:22-24** *That ye put off concerning the former conversation the old man, which is corrupt according to the deceitful lusts; And be renewed in the spirit of your mind; And that ye put on the new man, which after God is created in righteousness and true holiness.*

[17]**Exodus 20:3** *Thou shalt have no other gods before me.*

[18]**Joshua 24:15** *And if it seem evil unto you to serve the LORD, choose you this day whom ye will serve; whether the gods which your fathers served that were on the other side of the flood, or the gods of the Amorites, in whose land ye dwell: but as for me and my house, we will serve the LORD.*

[19]**Proverbs 11:1** *A false balance is abomination to the LORD: but a just weight is his delight.*

ARGUING AT THE DINNER TABLE

How do I Deal with Difficult People?

ೞ_____ ෨

The Lord is merciful and gracious, slow to anger, and plenteous in mercy...The mercy of the Lord is from everlasting to everlasting upon them that fear him, and his righteousness unto children's children;
Psalm 103:8,17

A new commandment I give unto you, that ye love one another, as I have loved you, that ye also love one another. By this shall all men know that ye are my disciples, if ye have love one to another.
John 13:34,35

Be not overcome of evil, but overcome evil with good.
Romans 12:21

"A man lives by believing something; not by debating and arguing about many things."
—Thomas Carlyle

Arguing is a waste of time and energy. People who know me know that. I don't like to dispute and I certainly don't like petty drama. I think if two people have a disagreement, they should be able to talk things out in normal tones and get to the bottom of it without holding grudges or slashing tires. *After all, we are Christians.* If anyone can handle controversy, we can. Our Head Honcho is Jesus the Christ—the One who is most famous for asking instead of arguing. We *should* be able to handle a little division without swinging pots and pans. But the truth is, I've been to a few church meetings in my day that prove otherwise. Yes, we *should* be able to sit down and have a polite conversation about politics without poking someone's eye out. But the truth is,

I know some people who wouldn't sing in the same choir as me if they knew who I voted for last year. They are Christians too.

Arguments have one intention in my opinion: to destroy happiness. A person who constantly argues is inwardly frustrated, and frustrated people are grumpy people. *Arguments. Yuck.* You show me an argumentative person and I'll show you an unhappy man. And not only an unhappy man, but an unhappy household. This is the cycle of an arguer. They try to make everyone else around them unhappy, and if it doesn't work, they keep digging at you until you blow up. Once you blow up, you start bickering mindlessly and finger pointing. Before you know it, you end up punching walls or jumping out of cars or screaming at your child or kicking the dog. *Poor dog.* All of these are telltale signs of unresolved frustration. So now, the whole family is frustrated because the arguer has provoked the argument. But by this time, he's somewhere sleeping and we're still arguing! Can't you see why I despise it? Arguing is too time-consuming and unnecessary. Two people screaming at each other only makes matters worse. It not only damages your vocal chords, but nobody can hear what the other person has to say. *Arguments.* Some people love it. Some people need it. Me? I don't like it one bit.

Now, not liking it doesn't mean that I *can't* do it. Oh trust me, I can argue. I just try not to. When I feel the fumes rising, I try to walk away and pray. That's what Jesus would do. When I start stuttering like Moses, I know something has plucked the bell tower of my heart. So, I try to apologize from the get-go before things are blown out of proportion. That's what Jesus would do. I find ways to fix a leak before the pipes are even broken. But, if none of these preventatives work, I argue.

Tonight was that kind of night. I had to defend myself. I had to speak up on the behalf of couples all around the world who aren't taken seriously. OK, maybe not all couples *(don't you just love when people make a global movement out of their personal madness?).* I had to speak up for me and Ana. I tried to avoid it, but before I knew it, I had tossed my "What Would Jesus Do" bracelet under the rug, slid into my imaginary boxing gloves and stepped into the ring.

In the words of Michael Buffer, "Let's get ready to rumble!"

ROUND 1:
THE ENGAGED COUPLE VS. THE MARRIED COUPLE

Ana invited me over to a friend's house. It was a couples gathering and, like always, we were the youngest. We talked and we talked and we talked. Subjects spanned from sports (I had nothing to say) to mortgage rates (still had nothing to say) and then, to God and marriage (bingo! Now I can participate). It was a nice and light conversation. Nothing to worry about. I was having a good time. And then, all of a sudden, someone asked THE question. The question of the season. The question of the hour. Every engaged couple gets it, and no one really wants to respond to it: "How do you feel?" *Typical question. Of course the women feel excited and the men feel reluctant. Of course, she has butterflies and he has the "I wonder why's?"* I was about to answer sarcastically and say, "Umm, I feel like I feel everyday, Pinky...I'm trying to take over the world!" But I didn't say that. These people didn't really know me. And frankly, they looked too saved to watch "Pinky and the Brain." So, instead of being humorous, I answered as nicely and as calmly as possible: "I feel like we're already married. I mean, it's no major difference in my mind because I've loved her and I have known her for a very long time. Five years to be exact." Wrong answer. I was hoping my response would cut away twenty minutes of back and forth yapping, coaching, and "you think you know but you have no idea" lecturing. It's funny. Every time older people talk to us about marriage, we feel like little children. We don't know what love is, we are too young to tell, and statistics state...blah, blah, blah. And then they turn around and tell us they got married at like 17. *Go figure.* I didn't want to argue, I promise. But this brother didn't care. He proceeded to interrogate me as if I were Sonia Sotomayor. No matter what I said, it wasn't sufficient. He had an argumentative disposition and would ask a question and then shoot back with a more complicated question. Just difficult. And to top it all off, he would cut me off in the middle of my sentence!

Now listen.

I'm OK with differing opinions. But please, please, don't cut me off. God is still working on me. Before I knew it, I was going back and forth with him. My heart was in the middle of the tennis court and we were slamming our verbal rackets at topnotch speed. I couldn't stop. I needed to win this match. I wanted to stop but my fans were holding up banners in the bleachers. I couldn't let them down.

"Sir, I'm a month away from getting married. If I don't begin to envision this thing as a reality, I will be shocked on the day after my wedding."

He replied, "Yes, but you're not officially married until the ceremony. You need this time to figure out if this is what you want."

I chuckled to myself. *If this is what I want? I've paid for the entire ceremony and the ring is halfway paid off. This better be what I want!* I tried to insert a laugh out loud in between the heated debate, but I wasn't laughing. Not at all.

Then he said it. Yes *it*: "You guys are so young. When I was your age, I was naïve too!" He looked over at his wife and she nodded in subtle agreement. I lost it. I stretched my racket back and struck that ball with all of my strength. I was so lost in the game that I didn't realize the fans were gone by this point. It was just me and him. Sweat streaming down our faces like the rushing waters of Niagara. Hearts bebopping to a tune too quick to measure; mine was about to flip out of my chest. *I'm asthmatic. But this is worth it.* Just me and Him. All the while, I'm pressing Ana's leg underneath the table to signal my frustration. *She's in pain. I'm heavy-handed.* She gets the hint and steps into the court midsentence.

"Time Out!" She exclaimed (at least that's what I heard in my imaginary tennis match).

I paused, took a sip of water, and then excused myself

from the table.

The night ended rather swiftly. We didn't wait for dessert and we didn't ask for coffee. We barely had time to grab our coats. We were in the car in less than 20 minutes. I sped home for no reason at all. I was hot, angry, and frustrated. I didn't know what to do. I didn't know what to say. And then, like a stage cue from heaven, Ana gently placed her warm hand on top of my swelling one. *Calmness entered the scene.* Seconds later, I was praying for him. I was praying for myself. I was asking God to open my eyes and close my mouth. Ana was God's instrument whether she knew it or not. Her touch silenced my frustration and calmed my inner storm. I slowed the car down and opened the door. I still don't know why I opened that door, but before I knew it, I was crying. On the side of the road, just crying. With tears streaming down my face, the Lord began to minister to me at the intersection. There were no audible words, but I heard God loud and clear. *Love Road and Mercy Avenue: the only way to deal with difficult people.* The words came to the forefront of my mind. They became my prayer and my lesson all in one. I prayed for God to help me with difficult people, and not before long, I was praying for the difficult person in me. For the frustration in me. For the unhappiness in me. The more I prayed, the more God planted in me the desire to read His Word.

I couldn't wait to get home. I knew there would be something in the Scriptures waiting for me. I felt God's presence through Ana's gentle touch, and I saw a reflection of my own unhappiness at the dinner table that night. I finally got home and flipped open the Bible. I didn't read it. I listened to it. The Spirit wanted to teach me about mercy. *Mercy. Of all things. Mercy.* The more I listened, the more I noticed a small but important revelation that I had never before considered. Surely, this little argument over dinner was set up for me to see up.

LOVING BEYOND LIP SERVICE

Jude 21 Keep yourselves in the love of God, looking for the mercy of our Lord Jesus Christ unto Eternal Life.

I want to talk about how to deal with difficult people the way Jesus dealt with them; that is, in a manner that is first loving, and second, merciful. If you reread the Scriptures listed at the beginning of this chronicle, you will find two words that are closely intertwined with one another—love and mercy. Now love and mercy are extremely popular words in church, but if you ask me, Christians juggle them around too loosely. We lack control and concentration. We say we love everything and we don't. We claim to love everyone and we lie. We can barely sit next to some people in church, and yet we love everybody? Doubtful. So love needs a facelift in our churches. We all agree. But if love needs a lift, then mercy needs mouth-to-mouth resuscitation. It is misused far more than love. For one, mercy only shows up to the party with her twin sister grace. And if grace is not mentioned, most people don't really know what to do with mercy. She's the silent sibling popularly known as "Grace's sister," but she doesn't have much personality alone. It reminds me of people at my school who say to Ana, "oh, you're Shaun's wife?" instead of asking "What's your name?" I find it hilarious and troubling at the same time. People would rather identify her by who she is related to, than show concern for her own individuality. I mean, yes, we are now officially married, but even before she knew me, Ana knew God. Ana was Ana. She was her own individual. Of course we are one in a spiritual sense, but we are not conjoined at the hip! We still have differences that shape our unity differently.

The same can be said about the grace and mercy unit. I can hear mercy agreeing, "Yeah. It would be nice if people were interested to know the differences between us." *Commercial Break.* It's a sad day in the world of relationships when a woman can't speak for herself. If you're connected to someone and you have no individual identity, you might need to step back and relearn your calling. Your Creator uniquely made you. You were not meant to be a clone of somebody else's original. You are not a shadow of someone else's image. You are not an extra in someone else's motion picture. You are exceptional all by yourself. The two of you make an even greater portrait, but remember, before he said, "I do," God called you, "good and very good." *Ok Shaun. Come back.* I'm back. So the mission of this section is to do just that. I don't want to file divorce papers or anything. I just want to highlight mercy for a moment and readjust our lenses so that we can place God's divine gifts in proper perspective.

First, know this. Mercy is not a one-dimensional term that simply means we get a pardon ticket from God in place of eternal damnation. I mean, that is an essential component of what mercy is, but it's not the be-all and end-all. Mercy is the expression of God's lovingkindness toward us. The gift is in the expression, not in the freedom ticket alone. The important word is expression. You know what an expression is; it's the shape that someone's face takes on. It's the look on somebody's face. The expression tells you how that person feels. The expression helps you to understand the words coming out of someone's mouth. So when I say mercy is God's expression, that means when God smiles, you don't see teeth; you see mercy. When God makes a motion in the Spirit, we see it displayed in the earth as mercy. We see God's face in mercy and we hear God's speech in love. Love is the language God speaks and mercy is the expression God makes.

Let me say it another way. Mercy is God's love packaged in noticeable signs. So if God shipped you a special delivery, the box you'd receive at the front door wouldn't be cardboard; it would be mercy. Why? Because mercy is the outermost layer of God's innermost love gift. It is a visible response to God's invisible love. It's one of the ways God shows us how much He loves us. It's tangible and visible and spiritual all at the same time. We can see it! We can touch it! We can sense it in the spiritual realm! He doesn't just forgive us and say, "Pay me back with your life." No, that would be something like divine imprisonment. Instead, God wraps His love in the package of mercy, and ships it to us as a "thank you" card from heaven. So, the only way we can open up God's love is if we first undo the wrapping paper of mercy.

Why is this important?

It's important because we need to see mercy in our lives before we can fully love difficult people. God's love toward us makes our love toward others possible. If you need a hint into God's love, start looking for mercy to show up in your life. That's what Jude 21 encourages us to do. It says, "Keep yourselves in the love of God, looking for the mercy of our Lord Jesus Christ unto Eternal Life." Start looking for mercy in everyday encounters. Pay attention to the cop who caught you speeding, and instead of giving you a ticket, he said, "Don't let it happen again." Pay attention to the teacher who offers you extra credit, even though you skipped class enough times to get an "F" for the year. See mercy in the man who ran out of the supermarket to give you the phone or purse you forgot. Remember the stranger who stopped you in the hotel lobby and said, "Maam, your headlights are still on." Yes, that's mercy. She saved you an entire day's worth of frustration and delay. You were moving too quickly to pay attention. You deserved a violation. You were about to lose your job and God saw fit to use people as messengers of His mercy. These are all expressions of God's love.

If you can't grasp this small but important nugget, then the next section will feel like you're learning a foreign language. The key is this: Mercy is not just a free pass out of detention. It is more like God's welcome letter into after-school tutoring. It is God's daily devotional from Him to us. It is God's love in action toward us, for us, by Him. In short, it is one of the most tangible ways to see and touch an intangible God. Mercy is so much more than you think!

How do I know? Well, if you look at the Hebrew word for

----------- ◈ -----------

Mercy is not subjective, exclusive, or preferential. We can't pretend to give love to church members but forsake our family members. That's not mercy at all; that's more like favoritism. When we begin to understand what mercy really encompasses, we will be able to love others beyond lip service.

----------- ◈ -----------

mercy, you'll find that it is the same word used to describe loving kindness. The word is *checed* in the Old Testament. When God shows checed in the Old Testament (248 times), you almost always see the word "mercy." And whenever you don't see mercy, you'll find *checed* translated as kindness or lovingkindness. So, the word 'love' and the word 'mercy' are interchangeable. You can't have love without having mercy. You can't separate love from mercy. The two are like Siamese twins. To love someone is to have mercy for them. It's just that clear-cut. We can't say we love our neighbor but yet we avoid them when we see them walking toward us in the grocery store. That's not love. That's lip service.

LOVING THE UNLOVABLE

Luke 6:32-33 For if ye love them which love you, what thank have ye? for sinners also love those that love them. And if ye do good to them which do good to you, what thank have ye? For sinners also do even the same.

Luke 6:35-36 But love ye your enemies, and do good, and lend, hoping for nothing again; and your reward shall be great, and ye shall be the children of the Highest: for he is kind unto the unthankful and to the evil. Be ye therefore merciful, as your Father also is merciful.

Now, I don't profess to be the smartest man alive, and I realize how naïve Ana and I may be, but one thing I know is this: love ain't love until you find yourself in an uncomfortable situation. Many times, I thought I was exercising love toward someone and I was actually just tolerating them. Or, I determined who got what based upon what someone did (or could do) for me. But this kind of attitude was not compassionate in nature. It was more like compensation.

The same can be said for many people reading, I think. If you're anything like me, you like to pick and choose who gets "love" and portion out who gets "mercy." There are only a few people in your phonebook who would get your last dollar, for instance. But this isn't the way Christ modeled love to us. Christ showed His love by giving mercy to people who would soon deny Him, betray Him and falsely accuse Him. Jesus loved the unlovable. That's the lesson of Luke 6. If you pay close attention to the Scriptures above, Jesus cleverly teaches *checed* by beginning the discussion on a subject titled "Easy love." He says that anyone can love a lovable person. That's easy. But who among you can love the difficult person? Who can give to the stingy, and do good to their enemy? Who can lend to broke folk and hope for nothing in return? Who among you? These were rhetorical questions with obvious answers. The answer was simple: no one can do such things. But this is exactly why Jesus entered the conversation this way. Beneath the surface of all of Christ's sayings and doings was the resolution to the problem: you can only love a difficult person through me (John 13:34; John 15:9).[1-2]

Jesus is teaching a new revised standard version of love. And then without warning, He replaces the word "love" with "mercy" before the listeners realize what's going on. Read verse 36 again. "Be ye therefore merciful, as your Father is merciful." Wait a minute, Jesus! You never introduced the word mercy. What are you doing here? It's precisely what I noticed about *checed* in the Old Testament. All along, Jesus was describing mercy by revising their idea of love. To love God's way is to love the unlovable. That's mercy. But, Jesus didn't speak in a way that would confuse them. He spoke their language and then changed their understanding. This was the secret behind Christ's masterful genius. *I wish more preachers would pay attention to the way Jesus taught.* He showed His disciples (by asking them clever questions) that what you call love and what I call mercy are one in the same. They are poured out from the same cup. They are variables in the same equation. Therefore, it is impossible to love God's way without including God's mercy within it.

Another example I use to explain this is that of purchasing a car with an extended warranty. An extended warranty goes beyond the period in which the car is new. And nine times out of ten, a new car won't need repair. So, the extended warranty comes in handy when the car has been stretched beyond its limitations. The extended warranty proves useful after the newness of the car wears off. In the same way, we don't need mercy when we are first introduced to someone. When people are new, they don't expose their defects. They are so easy to "love." *Insert violins and baby music.* But, after someone's newness wears off, you're going to wish you had that extended mercy to handle all of humanity's mechanical flaws. What are these flaws you ask? What do they look like? Good question. For one, these flaws become obvious to you when the brakes start wearing out in a relationship. You try to stop from arguing but you start squeaking. You know an "extended" season when you're in one. It usually begins after patience has ended. After that first argument, or during that first altercation at work, you will need something greater than you to say what you can't say alone. Initially, the boss thought you were a great employee until she realized you were next in line to take her job. Yup, that's when you need that extended warranty. And that husband was greater than vanilla ice cream until you realized he was spending all of your money without telling you. That's when you need that extended warranty. Oh, and that woman, she was your best friend until she listened to your heart long enough to steal your man. Uh huh, yeah, it's in the midst of these complex situations—that's when you realize what mercy is! This is what Jesus was saying in Luke 6. When you have all of the evidence to convict someone, and still, you decide to turn the other cheek, forgive them, and pray, you have stepped into the kind of love that only Jesus can give.

------------◈------------

Prayer: Lord, dress me in mercy. Layer me with Your lovingkindness. Help me to look like You. I now understand that man cannot love by words alone, but by every act of mercy that proceeds from God's expression in him.

------------◈------------

LORD, HELP MY TONE OF VOICE

Luke 6:7-8a And the scribes and Pharisees watched him, whether he would heal on the Sabbath day; that they might find an accusation against him. But he knew their thoughts…

Luke 6:11 And they were filled with madness; and communed one with another what they might do to Jesus.

We *should* have enough God within us to speak to everyone in a compassionate tone of voice, but when we are angry, we fail the test every time. Your tone of voice will speak louder than words themselves. Your silence, your screams, your short sentences—yes, they all speak louder than the cute words you say. You claim to be fine with your lips, but your tone gives it away every time (Proverbs 15:1).[3] I've even tried to email someone to avoid them hearing my voice, but even emails have a tone of their own! Text messages can be interpreted as short, mean, or offensive. You don't believe me? Try SENDING SOMETHING IN ALL CAPS TO SOMEONE and see what kind of response you will get.

Another section in Luke 6 teaches us to be mindful about our tone and response. It's found in the beginning of the chapter when the Pharisees try to catch Jesus healing on the Sabbath. Instead of getting angry, Jesus asks them a question: "… is it lawful on the Sabbath days to do good, or to do evil? To save life, or to destroy it? (Luke 6:9)[4] His question leaves them dumbfounded. Speechless. Scratching their heads. So while they are busy trying to decode Jesus' clever question, He restores the man's hand by saying, "Stretch forth thy hand…and his hand was restored as the other" (Luke 6:10).[5] Immediately, the Pharisees are filled with anger. They can't arrest him. They caught him but they can't arrest him. They witness Jesus revising the standard, but they can't punish him for doing a good deed.

Wow. Might I suggest that difficult people are mainly in your life to block you from restoring others around you? You think it's personal. But it's actually interpersonal. Difficult folk are not satisfied until you turn away from "withered hands" long enough to give attention to their vain babbling. As soon as the Christian family starts arguing outside, the news reporter ends up at the front door. Or, you have one debate about religion that makes you feel inadequate, so instead of obeying God, you stop writing the book. It's not personal. They want to stop your impact on the community. Don't you see it?

If you can learn from Jesus' example, you will not only avoid imprisonment, but you will heal the sick around you (even the Pharisees). So mind your tone of voice and don't let difficult people interrupt somebody else's healing process. Take your cue from Jesus. Try to respond with low tones and in a godly manner. But be very careful about what you call godly. A godly response and a churchy response are two different things. A godly response will set a difficult person on fire because he or she won't be able to irritate you beyond a certain point. Like Jesus, they will catch you but they won't be able to arrest you. A godly response will sound like Jesus. His tone (I imagine) and His clever response confused His enemies. You've got to learn how to listen to the intentions of your enemies and speak like Jesus. Jesus wasn't churchy and fake. He didn't start quoting a million Scriptures or screaming "the devil is a liar" at people with a frowned up face and some holy oil in his left hand. Please don't whip out the holy oil. Just speak to people in love. Trust me; your words will anoint more people in life than your hands will ever be able to touch.

------------ ◈ ------------

To have mercy is to love the unlovable and give to the stingy. That's totally opposite from what we're used to. But if love is never tested against difficult situations and people, are you certain that the love of God abides within you?

------------ ◈ ------------

EVERLASTING MERCY: THE MERCY THAT KEEPS ON GIVING

Psalm 103:17 But the mercy of the Lord is from everlasting to everlasting upon them that fear him…

So far, we have tried to get a better understanding of mercy and we've asked God to help our tone of voice. We've even learned how to look for mercy in all of the difficult places. But the question remains, how long should we be merciful? Isn't there a limit to this mercy stuff? A few days? A few months? I know the Bible tells us that His mercies are new every morning (Lamentations 3:22-23),[6] but that's God; not me. Doesn't mercy ever take a lunch break?

The Bible answers these questions in one simple word: everlasting. Psalm 103:17 offers a beautiful reminder to all of us, that, "the mercy of the Lord is from everlasting to everlasting." We would misrepresent Christ if we decided to give mercy one day and not give it the next. But, the beauty of this revelation lies in the fact that we can't access anything everlasting without God. It is God and God alone who has permanent access into everlasting things. God is an everlasting God, so everything God does is meant to last forever. He loves us with an everlasting love (Jeremiah 31:3),[7] He is the God of everlasting strength (Isaiah 26:4)[8] He is the God of everlasting life (Matthew 19:29)[9] God reigns with an everlasting righteousness (Psalm 119:142).[10] God can cast us into everlasting fire (Matthew 25:41).[11] Thus, God is the engineer of all things everlasting. We can't tap into anything everlasting on our own. We are finite, temporal, and human. But through Christ, we can do all things (Philippians 4:13).[12] If you let Him, God will teach you how to be eternally merciful the same way that He can give you everlasting life. Mercy is no exception.

------------ ◇ ------------

When you give consistent kindness to someone who does not deserve it——to someone about whom you have documented evidence that proves their guiltiness——and instead of convicting them, you show compassion toward them, you have walked into mercy everlasting.

------------ ◇ ------------

I am a living witness that God can make love so permanent in your life that when you try to erase it from the dry erase board, you won't be able to. The argument over dinner is just one example, but God has, on many other occasions, transitioned me from temporal toleration to everlasting love in seconds. And if the truth be told, God is continually working mercy in you, too. That's why you can't let your stubborn child go. God has placed everlasting mercy within you. That's why you can easily see beyond your loved one's flaws. God has planted a seed of mercy within, and the more you water it, the more it grows everyday. You wish you could blame yourself for other people's mistakes, but somehow God always reaches out to you and whispers, "This is not your fault." Those messages are small snippets of His everlasting mercy toward you.

------------ ◇ ------------

Merciful Redeemer, I'm so glad you never took a lunch break on me. Even in times of outright rejection, you chose to be merciful. Give me a dose of your everlasting love. Cure my love schizophrenia.

I want to treat everyone in a manner that reveals the Everlasting one within me. In Christ's Name. Amen

------------ ◇ ------------

JESUS TAKE THE WHEEL...BEFORE I CRASH!

Remember that difficult people come in a variety these days. Your difficult person could be an impatient drive-thru employee, an antagonistic in-law, or a telemarketer who just won't take no for an answer. She could be a new teacher at your job who thinks she knows it all, or your daughter who doesn't understand the value of a US dollar. The worst is when you're married to one! (Don't say AMEN too loudly). Yes, difficult people are diversely scattered around your life, but know this—they are all cured by the same spiritual medication: more love and extended mercy. Once you knock down the barrier with more love and extend mercy, you prove that Someone bigger than you is working inside of you. Don't allow what Paul calls "the carnal man" to overpower your Spirit man. When you sense that "old nature" rising up, and your reactions lean over to the fleshly "Shaun" and not the spirit-filled "Shaun" (replace my name with yours), try jumping directly into prayer (Matthew 26:41).[13] Prayer channels us to Jesus, and Jesus transforms our mind. Once the mind is transformed, our behaviors, our reactions, and our words change. Does that mean you have to pray aloud? Not necessarily. I've learned that you can quietly send signals to your mind that inform your flesh who the boss really is—the Spirit of God. The same way Mama knows how to shoot that one look across the room to get her daughter's attention, you can shoot one thought up to God and call things into divine order. This is prayer, too. You can rehearse a Scripture in your head without uttering a word. This is how you bring your body (and usually your tongue) under subjection to the Holy Ghost. Rehearsing, Rechanneling and Redirecting. That's what God has given us the power for. Once you do this, you are able to relax, assess the situation, and change the wind currents of the storm.

So, this rollercoaster of love has ended. I hope you can begin to answer the question, "How do we deal with difficult people?" But if you can't, let me offer one final concluding sentence: We deal with difficult people by allowing Jesus to take over when the situation gets too hard for us to handle ourselves. That's all folks. Difficult people need a dose of Jesus—and if you can't give it, move out of the way and let Jesus take over. Oh, and by the way, until you pass this test, it will just continue to repeat itself. So just deal with him. Deal with her. Deal with you. But when you do, make sure you deal with them at the corner of Love Road and Mercy Avenue.

------------ ◈ ------------

Prayer: Have mercy upon me O God, according to thy lovingkindness: according unto the multitude of thy tender mercies blot out my transgressions (Psalms 51:1). [14] *Meet me, Lord, by the riverbank. I want to give mercy, but first, help me to receive it. Help me to treat others the way You would treat them. Keep me in remembrance of thy word. A soft answer will turn, a merciful heart will give, and a loving spirit will forgive. Tear down the walls of pettiness. I want to be a living testament of your checed. Amen.*

------------ ◈ ------------

Practical Points

1

Difficult people are like an uninvited pimple. They pop up at unexpected places and show up on the most inconvenient day. But remember, you too were once as difficult as the person who is presently getting on your last nerve.

2

If you aren't at the place to extend love, walk away and pray off your steaming attitude. Pick up the Bible before you pick up the phone. Try not to call another friend immediately to vent. Try to pray it off. Write it out. Pray over what you write. Read it and release your frustration into God's hands. When the time is right, go back and handle the situation.

3 The challenge for every living Christian is to show God's love to the *entire* world on a consistent basis. This is why mercy is so difficult to do without Jesus. It's OK to call on Jesus in times of trouble; that's why He died. Don't worry about how difficult the situation is. In the face of difficulty, we get to see the reflection of Jesus most clearly.

4 Two quick minutes of lashing out could tarnish your testimony. Furious arguments are not worth it in the end. You have to go back to work tomorrow. You'll still be related to your family next year. Christ teaches us to love everyone. Even those who persecute you, annoy you, and are an aggravation to any conversation; we have a great commandment to love (Matthew 5:44).[15] It'll take a few lifetimes to master, but while we are here, we might as well try.

5 Like the energizer battery that keeps going and going and going, God is equipping you with the kind of mercy that will go with you forever. When you have mercy everlasting, you'll never be able to judge again. You'll only be able to extend and receive mercy from everyone you meet. To the woman, man, boy or girl who trusts God and gives mercy forever, God calls you blessed! (Matthew 5:7)[16]

Scripture Glossary

[1]**John 13:34** *A new commandment I give unto you, That ye love one another; as I have loved you, that ye also love one another.*

[2]**John 15:9** *As the Father hath loved me, so have I loved you: continue ye in my love.*

[3]**Proverbs 15:1** *A soft answer turneth away wrath: but grievous words stir up anger.*

⁴**Luke 6:9** *Then said Jesus unto them, I will ask you one thing; Is it lawful on the sabbath days to do good, or to do evil? to save life, or to destroy it?*

⁵**Luke 6:10** *And looking round about upon them all, he said unto the man, Stretch forth thy hand. And he did so: and his hand was restored whole as the other.*

⁶**Lamentations 3:22-23** *It is of the LORD's mercies that we are not consumed, because his compassions fail not. They are new every morning: great is thy faithfulness.*

⁷**Jeremiah 31:3** *The LORD hath appeared of old unto me, saying, Yea, I have loved thee with an everlasting love: therefore with lovingkindness have I drawn thee.*

⁸**Isaiah 26:4** *Trust ye in the LORD for ever: for in the LORD JEHOVAH is everlasting strength.*

⁹**Matthew 19:29** *And every one that hath forsaken houses, or brethren, or sisters, or father, or mother, or wife, or children, or lands, for my name's sake, shall receive an hundredfold, and shall inherit everlasting life.*

¹⁰**Psalm 119:142** *Thy righteousness is an everlasting righteousness, and thy law is the truth.*

¹¹**Matthew 25:41** *Then shall he say also unto them on the left hand, Depart from me, ye cursed, into everlasting fire, prepared for the devil and his angels:*

¹²**Philippians 4:13** *I can do all things through Christ which strengtheneth me.*

¹³**Matthew 26:41** *Watch and pray, that ye enter not into temptation: the spirit indeed is willing, but the flesh is weak.*

¹⁴**Psalm 51:1** *Have mercy upon me, O God, according to thy*

lovingkindness: according unto the multitude of thy tender mercies blot out my transgressions.

[15]**Matthew 5:44** *But I say unto you, Love your enemies, bless them that curse you, do good to them that hate you, and pray for them which despitefully use you, and persecute you.*

[16]**Matthew 5:7** *Blessed are the merciful: for they shall obtain mercy.*

CHRONICLES THAT *ENCOURAGE*

☙_____❧

REVIEWING MY SAVINGS ACCOUNT BALANCE

Still a Worshiper in a Spiritual Recession

℃_____℘

I will bless the Lord at all times...
Psalm 34:1

*A*ccording to the recent financial forecast, America is in an unprecedented recession. The nation is afraid and the people are panicking. Millions of people are losing their jobs. Fortune 500 businesses have filed bankruptcy and million-dollar homes are in foreclosure. Who would've ever thought this day would come? *I sure didn't.* America is the land of the free and the home of the brave. Free people get freer. They don't get bound again. Not like this. I never expected to wonder about whether I would have a job next year or not. I never worried about whether my financial aid package would be jeopardized before. Now I do. Now, I find myself worrying over things that were of no importance to me a year ago.

A year ago.

Just one year ago, I was working as a full time Teacher. Making good money. I was single, I was spending wisely, and I had no major bills. There was nothing to worry about. Just one year ago. And then along came recession—well, recession and my relocation from NJ to NC. Oh, and how could I forget...I got married. *That'll do it.* I went from living comfortably one day to living by faith every minute. Quickly. I'll never forget the first time I had to transfer money from my savings account. I said to myself, "This is only going to happen once." I was sure about it. I figured out when I would replace the money and everything. Then, two days later, I had to transfer again. Three minutes later, I had to transfer again. And before I knew it, I was completely transferred out. No more monkeys jumping on the bed. No more oodles and noodles under the kitchen cabinet—*I always seemed to run out of those when I actually have a taste for them.* All I had saved up for a rainy day was spent out for a stormy night.

SEEING GOD IN THE ECONOMIC RECESSION

"Recession turns peoples lives upside down. It helps them realize that they don't have a sufficiency unto themselves."
—*Michael Bell*

Luke 15:14 And when he had spent all, there arose a mighty famine in that land; and he began to be in want.

Has anyone in your close circle been affected by this recession? Have only bad things come out of it? If someone has come to God as a result of this recession, then I think God is totally behind it. Remember the story of the prodigal son? He is the younger brother in one of Jesus' parables who demands his allowance from his father and soon flees home to live the good life. Interestingly enough, two things happen after he spends all that he has. First, the famine comes. Then, he begins to want. Now. The famine back then represented something similar to a recession nowadays. It was a drought. No more family vacations. A limited potluck for Thanksgiving. Maybe one gift for Christmas instead of two; and don't you dare ask for a new pair of sneakers in the spring. We're in a famine.

Whenever famines happened in the land, no one was happy about it—especially broke folks. And this brother is so broke, he's willing to eat pig food for dinner (Luke 15:16).[1] *Yuck.* But, not only does the famine interest me here. The timing of it all strikes me as important to discuss as well. The son begins to want after he spends his allowance entirely. Isn't that interesting? Pre-

[1] Bell, Michael. "How the Recession May Fuel Church Growth." <u>Eclectic Christian</u>. 14 Oct. 2009. *http://eclecticchristian.com/2009/04/06/how-the-recession-may-fuel-church-growth/*

famine, the son doesn't really want anything. He just wastes his allowance away. But, after he loses what he once had, then he wants everything that he can no longer obtain. *Pause. Don't play with what God has entrusted to you. You may start wanting what you willingly gave up after it's all out of your control. Unpause.* So, God allows this famine to happen so that, eventually, the son would return home to His father. It's the hunger, desire, and the unquenchable thirst that motivates the prodigal son to actually "come to himself" and turn from his wicked ways (Luke 15:17).[2] There was a purpose behind it. That's my point. And the same is true during this season of recession. God would never allow this to happen at this magnitude unless there was a purpose beyond the problem. God knows that some of us won't turn around until the thing we love fails us. God knows that we often only turn to Him after the carpet has been pulled out from under us. God knows that. He even knows that some people will *never* approach Him until they realize how bad they need Him. So, sometimes, God mismatches socks in our personal lives in order to get our spiritual life in order. God doesn't fix it; God just fixes us. And instead of fixing the famine, God uses the unexpected circumstance to deepen our trust in Him and to communicate His unfailing love toward us.

This is the perfect opportunity to hear God calling your name. He's been calling you your entire life, Mr. or Mrs. Prodigal, but you've been too distracted by livelihood to receive Life. The normal routine has budgeted God out of the bottom line, and still, God knocks on the door of your heart. Does it have to get any worse for you to obey Him?

------------ ◈ ------------

Sometimes we only feel the pressure of recession when it knocks on our front door. When someone in our household loses a job or when our pension is taken away, then we think about going back to church. If God is using this recession to reposition you, then let God do what God wants to do.

------------ ◈ ------------

RED ALERT: A CONGREGATIONAL RECESSION

"One of the biggest problems is that we aren't transparent and critically reflective in many churches. We hide behind masks, as if we were all in theatre, and then refuse to ponder the complexities of our frail human existence."
—CJ Rhodes

This economic recession is also a modern-day parable for the spiritual recession going on. I don't know if you realize it or not, but almost every Christian I know has felt, at some point this year, a bit recession'ish. *You know the feeling.* Something is happening and you don't know how to stop it. You wake up. You start your car. You drive off to go to work. Everything is normal. The same as yesterday. Ten minutes later, you're on the highway, and you hear a click. There's something underneath the car making a familiar noise, but you keep driving because you've become numb to it. You're numb to almost everything nowadays. Your car didn't sound this way when you bought it off the lot, but it's nothing major; besides, life is too busy for you to stop and get a mere clicking sound checked out. There are too many church services to go to. Too many people need you. You were once a friend. Now you have become their Messiah. You? Don't worry about you. You'll be fine. It's only a car.

Ten minutes later, your car begins to thump. Thumping turns into pounding, and pounding turns into chuckling. You put on the hazards. Cars are zooming along. No one wants to let you over. You break down in the middle of the highway. You're spiritual battery is drained. You can't step out on the highway or else you will die. Someone will hit you. *Doesn't anyone see my hazard lights?* You can't access help. Today of all days, your phone is dead. You're in church, singing with the choir. *Dead.* Spiritually checked out. Everyone else is busy praising God. You? You're just going through the motions and praying that no one will see the pain, sense the fear, or read the "I give up" sign written across your forehead.

Saints, the Body of Christ is breaking down before our eyes and I need to know if anyone sees it happening besides me. It does not make sense for us to question how we got here or even why we got here. We just need to realize that there's been a spiritual shift and we need to do something about it. Just look around. On the whole, American Christianity is on life support. Instead of getting better, we're getting worse. We procrastinate, we're lazy, we're consumed with work or church, and our family time is shrinking by the day. Our carnal man is trying to squeeze the new creature into old clothes. Clothes we can't stand anymore. Clothes we can't fit anymore. We're picking up bad habits that we threw away years ago and experimenting with things we vowed never to try.

And why? Who knows? You don't even know for sure. All you know is that you're losing steam, and you're transferring money out of the savings account to cover the costs but you're not making up for it. So all you do now is reflect on how things used to be or how you wish things could be. *Regret and reminiscence will destroy your future goals if you let them.* It's the same old sad song. Your relationship with God was once so vibrant and flourishing. Your prayer life was so fruitful and fulfilling. Church used to be so rejuvenating and empowering. *Once upon a time.* Then you start wondering if God even loves you anymore. You feel like

> *On the whole, American Christianity is on life support. Discernment has seemingly left the building. Fewer children go to church and fewer adults are open about their Christianity. In fact, the majority of people who do go to church, either come out of obligation or habit.*

you've failed Him one too many times. You think joining a new church will do the trick, and when you get there you find out that they are just as depleted as the church you left. You're stagnant, you're weighed down, and all of this came over you unexpectedly. In your mind, your car trouble came out of nowhere. But from the Mechanic's point of view, you should've seen this coming as soon as you heard the clicking noise. You were freely worshiping last year. Now, you're going through the motions. Just one year later. *Isn't it amazing how seconds between worship and worry, you can shift from "I believe God" to "God isn't real?"* You look around. Then, you close your eyes trying to block everyone out. They think you're worshipping, and you're actually contemplating suicide. Everyone around you is acting as if they are OK, so you join the crowd. Pretending. Unfocused. Stuck. Again. *How did this happen to me again?* Stuck in recession. Stuck without an explanation or a desire to be here again. You don't even enjoy the quick fixes anymore. Stuck in the middle of the road with hazard lights on, and you look around and think to yourself, "Will anyone on this highway ever discern where I am, slow down and help me out?" Indeed, the congregation is in a spiritual recession!

PERSONAL RECESSION:
THE ME THAT NOBODY SEES

But not only is the congregational church in a recession. The people within the church are in individual recessions. *Somebody please tell me:* What am I supposed to do when I find myself in a spiritual recession? The church has nothing to do with this one. It's me. I have no resources left. I can't reach into my savings account for a transfer. I need restoration. I need to cry. I need God to hug me. I'm weak. But, I don't tell anyone I'm weak and I certainly don't tell anyone when I'm broke. Why? Well... because I'm ashamed. My spirit is in foreclosure again, and I'm the pastor. My spirit is in foreclosure, and I'm the Youth President. My spirit is in foreclosure and I'm the leader of the dance team. How did this happen? The people around me don't know it and I plan to keep it that way. I'll just take more medication. That'll do the trick.

No. That will not do the trick. More medicine will only make you feel like everything will pass, but I'm writing to tell you, it won't. I may not be able to aptly speak about the economic recession or even the congregational one, but I hope I can offer some words of encouragement for those in a personal recession. I need you to understand this if you don't understand anything else. Every member in the body of Christ is experiencing something intense right now. This is the season of intense warfare and overturn. The hands, the arms, the leg—EVERY MEMBER. You are not alone. You are not odd. Some of us have a better way of covering it up—and others of us are deceiving ourselves. You're stuck now, but you definitely won't be stuck forever.

The only way to get out of this slum is to worship through the famine. Worship through the pain. Worship in spite of the emptiness. That's my reflexive answer. But I know what your response is. *Easier said than done.* Right? Right. That's what I would've said. So, I've decided to show you better than I can tell you. I've decided to walk you through what I mean by exposing a page out of my own recession book. I'm going to share my diary with you.

Now listen. I hesitated over whether or not to include this in the chronicle. I wrestled with it because, from my observation, most church leaders and devotional writers are so polished and encouraging—always—and to be quite honest, I didn't want to be the exception. *Pride. I'm guilty of it as well.* But, then I thought about Mahatma Gandhi's famous quote, "Be the change you want to see." And rarely (if ever) do I see the behind-the-scenes drama before the actors come out on the stage and shout me to excitement. Yes, they preach an excellent sermon, they sing a powerful song, and they share a wonderfully edited testimony. But, rarely do I hear my leader's open struggles with life on a day-to-day basis. *Yet we all struggle with life. Go figure.* We don't see when the worship leader reaches for the bottle instead of the Bible. We don't hear about the nights they stay awake trying to "put the flesh to sleep"—only to give in to temptation, and battle with feelings of unworthiness all over again. We don't see it, and if we do catch wind of it, we gossip about it. We don't pray. We don't cover each other. And as a result, our preachers become closeted Christians. They don't want to reveal their real-life uncertainties for fear of you judging them, so they keep it hidden in their closet. They don't want to be exposed and humiliated, so they keep it tucked away in a locked file on their computer. *That computer can be a dangerous device after 11 PM; but anyway*— They don't want to tell the whole testimony; no, that would ruin their self-glory. And neither did I. But then I realized, this is exactly what God *needed* me to do. This is why God called me to write: to resist the impulse to be seen by others as better, wiser, smarter, and more spiritual.

May my recent diary entry comfort someone who has had a recession day like this before.

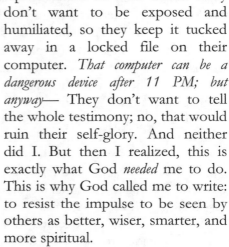

The most effective sermons will touch reality with the fingertip of God's anointing. The best meditations are not those that allow us to escape into Never-never land, but those that teach us to confront the issues that will not go away even after we've spoken in tongues for hours on end.

July 4, 2009 6:38 AM- I feel like I'm drowning.

Today is somber and cloudy. I wake up this morning and I want to pray. Alone. I bend down and try to begin my prayer with a million and one things to say. My mental car is crashing into the brick wall of delusion and sadness. I can't even get out a good sentence. I can't focus my mind on anything. I start thinking about how much I really don't want to write this book. The deeper I get into trying to explain the things that most people would hate to read, the more discouraged I become. I'm fighting that. I'm fighting the question of graduate school and/or publication work. I'm fighting it hard. My head hurts. And then, of course, I'm fighting me. I'm fighting my fears. Am I hitting against the prick? Am I trying to complicate the will of God? Am I just being difficult for no reason at all? Shaun, just let it go and trust God. I'm trying.

July 18, 2009 6:00 PM- Say something encouraging. Cant.

Went to barbershop today.   My barber started talking about marriage.   Great. Another conversation about marriage.   He begins, "Man, sometimes I just don't want to do it." I respond, "I hear you, man." He continues, "Because women don't understand, I like to have my space, man." I acquiesced.   He continued, "And I'm the kind of person who is adventurous. I'll just drive to New Jersey tonight and be back to work by Monday morning." I reacted, "Wow! We're a lot a like." We bonded and we joked, but I didn't have an ounce of hope in me to encourage him.   He hinted at marital problems and I had no testimony to help him overcome. I had no anecdote to get him to focus on something else. No cute analogy. No word of advice.

I was on empty.

July 22, 2009 8:40 AM- I'm tired of praying and getting nowhere.

Got dressed and went to favorite breakfast spot. The lady served me sweet tea without a straw. Major problem. I sat there unhappy, cold, and thirsty — quickly realized: I'm longing for something more than a quick beverage. Something more than a nice meal. I'm yearning for answers. Answers to this complex equation called life. Answers to this roadmap with several landmarks but few destination points. Why does the church always point me toward what I'm going to get later? I need answers today. I can't go on like this. I need answers. Not philosophical, existential, psychological, or any other –ogical answers. I need GOD to speak to me. Tried to pray. Couldn't find the words to say. God's not talking much today. Maybe this stuff isn't as real as they say it is. I've got to get back on the worship treadmill and burn off the fat I've accumulated since I've been stagnant and distracted. Maybe later. I'm going back to sleep.

July 22, 2009 8:42 AM- Can't sleep.

I can't stay asleep all day. I gotta get up. I wake up to more questions and fewer answers. I tried praying again. No words. No songs. No inspiring intellectual revelations. I'm tired. Really tired. But, Shaun, you just slept. Oh that's right. Get out of the bed, walk over to the bus stop, and keep it moving.

I soon realize that no buses are running today. So, I walk. Two minutes later, God sprinkles my head with droplets of precipitation. Wait. Now a downpour of heavy rain. Wait. This rain isn't stopping. Didn't the songwriter say the storm is passing over? Well, why is it still raining then?!? Great.

No words to say. No umbrella to protect me. No bed to hide under. No monster under my bed to blame. No straw in my tea. And I'm soaking wet.

I walk and walk and walk. I look behind me, hoping for a bus to come and rescue me. I look in front of me, hoping for a——I don't know what I was hoping for——maybe a familiar face to ask if I needed a ride. I look down at my phone, hoping for a text message to distract me. I need a job to run to...or run away from, a friend to encourage (because I tend to hide my pain behind others), a task to complete for someone else, anything——just give me anything so I can distract myself from me; from dealing with the awkwardness of a day I didn't predict; a rainstorm I wasn't properly dressed for——I need something or someone to give purpose to my mind's exasperation. If I find something to do, then I can do it until I grow tired, and then I can fall asleep and start the wheel of life over again tomorrow.

To no avail. No buses drove by, no cars beeped, no texts were sent, no one else's day is as cloudy as mine. Great. I have to confront me. I have to confront the silence.

July 22, 2009 9:05 AM- Dear Lord, it's me again.

I finally utter five words to God: "Dear Lord, it's me again." I exhale. That's it. My entire prayer today. "Dear Lord, it's me again." I wish I could say

I spoke an eloquent prayer or traveled into another realm of prayer (wherever that is), but I didn't. I was too distracted by the sound of my own unfamiliar voice. I couldn't say anything more. The weight of words and speechlessness compressed me 'round about. I had so much to say but I couldn't find any words to perfectly express this pain. This distance. This void. I felt trapped into silence like a woman trapped in an abusive relationship; or a prisoner trapped inside of his cell; or a slave trapped in someone else's cotton field. Trapped. By my own silence. I knew if I started talking, my sentence wouldn't end.

Dear Lord, It's me again.

Nothing else to say after that. I was speechless. The one who writes daily devotionals like they're going out of style, and the one who composes 100 songs a year that (maybe) only 30 people will ever hear; the one who has volumes of unfinished books in his computer——speechless.

The one who always has something to say to encourage someone else, had nothing to say to encourage himself. I didn't even remember to say "Amen." That's the professional way to do this prayer thing, right? But today, I ain't wanna be professional.

July 22, 2009 9:15 AM- Still walking in the rain.

Still walking. Still raining. Still hurting. The complex simplicities of life, the yin and the yang, the crystal stair came crashing down on me. I was underneath it. I suddenly felt the shatters of glass lodged deeply into the outer layers of my skin. Ouch. I needed answers. NOW!

The lingering and longing and hiding away of life's misplaced modifiers caused this unending tragedy to play its final selection in today's production. "Dear Lord, it's me again." Shaun, cut it out! You're being dramatic. You've got two hands, two feet, two eyes...ya know, the 'I won't complain' thing used to really work. It used to snap me out of things and I would get myself together quickly; that is, until I realized that I had too many two's and not enough one's; too many bones and not enough chicken; I'm too skinny, I'm not smart enough, I'm not sure what my future looks like. Too many choices and still, not enough options.

Answer. Me. "Dear Lord, it's me again."

I just wanted Him to know that I was around His altar, sitting on His lap, knocking on His door, listening to His birds and feeling His beautiful rain on my cheek——oh no, those were tears. Well, it all starts to feel the same after you've cried an ocean in the middle of a desert. I wanted Him to know that I loved Him, that I chose Him (I think), and I wanted Him to love me back. It was like approaching the girl of your dreams, but you were too shy to tell her how you felt since that same girl saw you fall down the 2nd floor staircase after the student government meeting; she saw you walk headfirst into a pole after school, and she caught you spill your food on the principal's new suit. Why can't I get it right! She saw you at your ugliest——surely, she wouldn't be attracted to you. Yes, that was how it felt. I felt like the child who was punished by her mom and she knew that the school dance was tomorrow night. So, she sneaks into the kitchen to ask for permission to go out with her friends (knowing her mom would scream, 'Go to your room!'). Yes, that's how I felt. I felt like I had argued with my wife and then I had to initiate the first, "I'm sorry." Yes, that's how I felt. I couldn't utter words. I just hoped that somehow, God would understand me in my silence. I wanted to feel His active and abundant life inside of the agony and antipathy of my own. I wanted God to know that even in this somber day, I was still there—— here——anywhere He was. No straw. No umbrella. No text messages. But I was here. I still desired to be included in His holy witness protection plan, but I didn't know if I qualified anymore.

Dear Lord, It's me again.

It was an invitation for God to see me peek through the inner courts of glory, longing for Him to turn around and grab me, hug me tightly, and say those beautiful words, "I forgive you." And in some clever way, He did. I looked up to the sky and all of a sudden, the rain ceased. The bus appeared and the text messages flooded my phone as if someone had been holding them hostage until God and I shared our brief eternal moment. I felt an embrace that I can't quite describe. I felt the calmness of the storm and experienced the rainbow of assurance through the subtle whispers of Psalm 23:

> The LORD is my shepherd; I shall not want.
> He maketh me to lie down in green pastures:
> he leadeth me beside the still waters.
> He restoreth my soul:

Wow. My soul was in need of deep restoration.

July 22, 2009 9:20 AM- On the bus now

I realize what happened now. Anxiety over tomorrow had captivated my thoughts. I was trapped in the claustrophobia of failure.

All I knew best was how not to succeed. But, God freed me with His Word. He's my shepherd. That's what I'm going to hold onto today.

He's leading me. He's guiding me. Before the waters could be still, they first had to be troubled. He leads me beside the still waters and makes me to lie down.

I don't know if "He makes me to lie down" means God forced me down or that He invited me to lie down. I don't care about Hebrew transliteration today. I just know that I'm lying down. I'm riding on the bus but I'm lying down. I'm gripped tightly in the bosom of El Shaddai. I'm closer to God in the downpour than I am in the sunshine. I feel Him. In the rain. I feel Him on my head. I see His presence on my wet jeans.

God is still with me.

MY HEART AND ALL THE CONFUSIONS THEREIN

There you have it—my heart and all the confusions therein. I want you to know that I struggle just like you. I wonder and I wander just like you. I experience seasonal shifts just like you. And most importantly, I experience recessions just like you. So, whenever you find yourself in a famine, take a walk and worship God. Don't allow your spiritual automobile to break down in the middle of the road. Too many souls are connected to the church's final destination; and God is working out His mission in you.

Wake up.

Walk out.

Worship.

Allow God to fix the clicking sound in your life, and then, after God has fixed you, go and help fix someone else. Restore your brother or sister next to you (Luke 22:32).[3] Don't leave half of the members discouraged, diseased or destroyed. Feel one another's burdens (Galatians 6:2).[4] Respond to other people's pains—even if you are the cause of that pain. As a body, we must be more discerning than we are suspicious, and more concerned than we are nosy. We must abide in God day in and day out (John 15:10).[5] Prayer warriors need to assume position. Youth leaders need to bring the children together. Pastors should meet and counsel one another. Gossiping will be of no benefit and a personal day, cutting class, or vacation won't fix this. We need to apply spiritual things to a spiritual situation. We need to worship, edify one another by the Word of God, and listen. Listen to what the Spirit is saying to the church (Revelation 2:29).[6] Listen to the people. Just listen. The pains of the people are screaming. Shame is screaming. Silence is screaming. We must be still and listen.

WHAT DO I DO IN A RECESSION? WORSHIP & PRAY

Hebrews 7:24-25 But this man, because he continueth ever, hath an unchangeable priesthood. Wherefore he is able also to save them to the uttermost that come unto God by him, seeing he ever liveth to make intercession for them.

Remember, you are still a worshipper even in a spiritual recession! Don't forget it. Worship is crucial during economic, congregational, or personal recessions. When we worship, we hit the refresh button on our Internet browsers. We see the same page but with different updates. When we worship, it's almost like applying remover onto that spicy red nail polish. At first, it will be difficult to rub off, but if you keep on rubbing, after a while, the remover of His presence and the memory of His blood will purify all stains of guilt. Just worship! Use the gifts that God has given you and work the works of Him who sent you (John 9:4).[7]

Worship not because you know what's going on, but precisely because you don't. And as you worship, remember to pray with understanding (1 Corinthians 14:15).[8] Worship is where we can empty out and receive strength but prayer is where we are shaken and

------------◈------------

Prayer is that place where we see God face to face. Prayer is that earthly occasion where Jesus' heavenly occupation as Lead Intercessor is realized. In prayer, we struggle as unholy and imperfect people to speak to a holy and perfect God. Yet, we have the grace to enter boldly before the throne because Jesus is always interceding for us. (Hebrews 4:16; 7:24-25). [9-10]

------------◈------------

reassured. Pray because prayer helps us navigate through life's problems. Worship because worship helps the mind to submit to the mind-maker. As Karl Barth once put it, when we pray, we are able to "pray through the mouth of Jesus Christ," withholding nothing. And I would add, when we worship, God is able to pastor us through perplexing pastures and preach to us through our own worshipful confessions. *Has it ever happened to you? It's happened a million times to me.* The best sermons are given to us out of our own desperate cries and the best songs are composed after we have dealt with our own silent storms. When we finally enter in, we are positioned back into alignment with God. *Just try it.* Worship and pray. Pray and worship.

ON PUNISHMENT FROM THE TEMPLE

"When you can't find the words to say and everyone else has already written you off, get in the position of worship."
—*Donnalee Donaldson*

For my worship leaders out there, this final section is for you. Many of us worship leaders think that in order to write a worship song, we must create a deep prayerful presence and have every part of our lives so pristinely consecrated that God himself would live in us if He were to come back for a sequel visitation. Quite on the contrary, two of David's top ten hymn-psalms "Create in Me" (Psalm 51:10)[11] & "As the Deer" (Psalm 42:1)[12] were written after sinful pleasure conceived death of father and illegitimate son (2 Samuel 12:9)[13] and *while* David was in exile from the temple (the place where he commonly worshiped). So, get this. While David was on punishment from the temple, he was still able to write a song that pierced his heart and softened God's. He welcomed us 21st Century Christians into his bedroom of affliction and invited us to lay on the table as he received open heart-surgery from Dr. God. Exposed, painful, not cute. King David was in a recession. David could not go to the temple, but that restriction taught him to look inwardly to the temple inside of him (1 Corinthians 6:19).[14] He couldn't sing with instruments so he sang with humming birds and whistling winds. It wasn't while he was in the spirit on the Lord's day. No. Those moments (where the glory fills the temple) typically provoke silence and awe, not psaltery and harp. Rather, it was while David was enduring exile. Recession. Loss. Pain. That was when God used him to reform our understanding of worship.

This should be an encouragement to you. What you're going through is *transformational.* You've been handpicked by God to shine a new light on God's mystery. So, keep on writing. Keep on singing. Continue to worship in your wilderness. David teaches us that the best and truest worshiper writes her best song in the middle of disaster, approaching reprobation, "prodigaling" through the forest of her innermost doubts and fears. This is where she pens the true essence of her heart and God shows up to sign His name on her composition.

I encourage you to worship during your spiritual recession. It's never inappropriate to worship God, and it will truly transform your perspective and bring clarity to the purpose of this season in your life.

SHALL WE CONTINUE IN SIN? GOD FORBID.

And for all of us who are in a recession (not just musicians and singers), permit me to encourage you, too. I know you may be struggling, but be encouraged. Struggles are a sign of success, not failure. The struggle enlists us as one of God's own. It is a sign that something within us is allergic to the old men/women we used to be (2 Corinthians 5:17).[15] Furthermore, the fact that we wrestle with God is a sign of strength, not a sign of weakness. It is our evidence that our Spirit screams "Yes" louder than the whisper of our flesh, which will forever utter "no."

No one who will ever do anything significant for God is exempt from struggle. In fact, to cease from struggling is to cease from living in Christ. It is through struggle, my friends, that worship is defined; that our purpose in this world is clarified. Our struggles produce better worshipers out of us in the end. Why? Because struggle is not solely about suffering; it is also about the resurrection.

Now, allow me to clarify something here. I am not cheering on backsliders and I am not advocating sin. I am simply rethinking the purpose of struggle. I know that Paul asks, "Shall we continue in sin? God forbid" (Romans 6:1).[16] But I also know that God is married to the backslider. (Jeremiah 3:14).[17] Therefore, I am encouraging you to give thanks even in the midst of your deepest "struggle." *I don't know. I can't explain it.* But it's something about being in the shadows of sin and singing, "Lord You are Holy" that shakes the foundation of what I once thought holiness was. It is something about worship on the unemployment line that differentiates the true worshiper apart from the talented singer. It's something about being amidst a congregation of vocal geniuses, and having your non-harmonious screams reach heaven because of your broken spirit and contrite heart (Psalm 51:17).[18] It's just something about a worshipful decision that produces a worshipful heart, and a worshipful heart that will inspire a worshipful decision.

I encourage you, wherever you are, to hold up your head up and whisper "Yes" to God. Make a decision to bless the Lord even in the chaos and even in the recession. Will you *decide* to bless the Lord with me? All times means all times.

------------◈------------

Christianity is about God loving us. Worship is about us loving God. Worship is an active life decision. It is my "no" from those toxic relationships, habits, and cravings. It is my "yes" to honor, serve and praise the Lord. The man who is in love with God reveals his passion by giving himself wholly to Jesus, forsaking all else just to hear God whisper back sweet nothings.
This is why we love God, even in a spiritual recession.

------------◈------------

Questions for Introspection
ᢙ_____ᢛ

1) Do you believe that communities all across the world are returning to God because of this recession? If so, what are you doing to evangelize and serve Christ? What can your church do?

2) Where is your secret place? When is the last time you worshipped there?

Practical Points

1 David is revered because of his passion for God, his repentant posture and his willingness to fix things after he made huge mistakes. His transparency helps us realize, "I'm not the only one." If this chronicle is speaking to you, have faith in God and worship through your recession. You are not the only one. Let God do what God wants to do and don't blame Wall Street. When we blame greedy humans and point the finger toward the government, we miss what the Spirit could be saying to the church.

2 Every good painting needs a shadow of gray, and yet, so many Christian leaders fear exposing their wrinkles to others. Don't get caught up in masking so that others *think* you are perfect. We are not called to be Superheroes. We are called to take up our cross and follow Christ. Christ is the real Hero, not you. The more you hide your uncertainties, the greater the possibility that others will idolize your seeming perfection.

3 When you realize that tomorrow's worries are sliding into today's agenda, stop what you're doing and just take a walk. Walk out your worries and sorrows. Cry if necessary. Talk to God even if you can only utter five words. And then, listen to the silence.

4

Stay alert so that no one around you gets smothered in mud by this tug-of-war battle. Tell your flesh "NO!" Awaken the Spirit of God in you and don't let her go back to sleep. When you get weak (because you will), drop pride and find someone in whom you can confide to pray with you. Accept the fact that God loves you and challenge yourself to become a better person because of it.

5

If we allow our state as sinners to overwhelm us, we will never do a work for God. We will always live as if Jesus didn't die, and we'll look to other imperfect humans for resolution. The key to deliverance is not the cover up, it is genuine repentance. It is not flawlessness; it is conviction. Woe be unto that man who says he hasn't sinned (1 John 1:8).[19] Move forward. Repent. Get Up. Work! (Romans 8:1; Galatians 5:1; 2 Corinthians 5:17)[20-22]

Scripture Glossary

[1]**Luke 15:16** *And he would fain have filled his belly with the husks that the swine did eat: and no man gave unto him.*

[2]**Luke 15:17** *And when he came to himself, he said, How many hired servants of my father's have bread enough and to spare, and I perish with hunger!*

[3]**Luke 22:32** *But I have prayed for thee, that thy faith fail not: and when thou art converted, strengthen thy brethren.*

[4]**Galatians 6:2** *Bear ye one another's burdens, and so fulfil the law of Christ.*

[5]**John 15:10** *If ye keep my commandments, ye shall abide in my love; even as I have kept my Father's commandments, and abide in his love.*

[6]**Revelation 2:29** *He that hath an ear, let him hear what the Spirit saith unto the churches.*

[7]**John 9:4** *I must work the works of him that sent me, while it is day: the night cometh, when no man can work.*

[8]**1 Corinthians 14:15** *What is it then? I will pray with the spirit, and I will pray with the understanding also: I will sing with the spirit, and I will sing with the understanding also.*

[9]**Hebrews 4:16** *Let us therefore come boldly unto the thrown of grace, that we may obtain mercy, and find grace to help in time of need.*

[10]**Hebrews 7:24-25** *But this man, because he continueth ever, hath an unchangeable priesthood. Wherefore he is able also to save them to the uttermost that come unto God by him, seeing he ever liveth to make intercession for them.*

[11]**Psalm 51:10** *Create in me a clean heart, O God; and renew a right spirit within me.*

[12]**Psalm 42:1** *As the hart panteth after the water brooks, so panteth my soul after thee, O God.*

[13]**2 Samuel 12:9** *Wherefore hast thou despised the commandment of the LORD, to do evil in his sight? thou hast killed Uriah the Hittite with the sword, and has taken his wife to be thy wife, and hast slain him with the sword of the children of Ammon.*

[14]**1 Corinthians 6:19** *What? know ye not that your body is the temple of the Holy Ghost which is in you, which ye have of God, and ye are not your own?*

[15]**2 Corinthians 5:17** *Therefore if any man be in Christ, he is a new creature: old things are passed away; behold, all things are become new.*

[16]**Romans 6:1** *What shall we say then? Shall we continue in sin, that grace may abound?*

[17]**Jeremiah 3:14** *Turn, O backsliding children, saith the LORD; for I am married unto you: and I will take you one of a city, and two of a family, and I will bring you to Zion.*

[18]**Psalm 51:17** *The sacrifices of God are a broken spirit: a broken and contrite heart, O God, thou wilt not despise.*

[19]**1 John 1:8** *If we say that we have no sin, we deceive ourselves, and the truth is not in us.*

[20]**Romans 8:1** *There is therefore now no condemnation to them which are in Christ Jesus, who walk not after the flesh, but after the Spirit.*

[21]**Galatians 5:1** *Stand fast therefore in the liberty wherewith Christ hath made us free, and be not entangled again with the yoke of bondage.*

[22]**2 Corinthians 5:17** *Therefore if any man be in Christ, he is a new creature: old things are passed away; behold, all things are become new.*

TURNING THE JUMP ROPE

I, too, Have a Dream: Until we all Come Together

ɔઅ_____ઝɔ

Till we all come in the unity of the faith, and of the knowledge of the Son of God, unto a perfect man, unto the measure of the stature of the fullness of Christ.
Ephesians 4:13

For where two or three are gathered together in my name, there am I in the midst of them.
Matthew 18:20

*I*t's a bright and windy autumn day. I'm driving across town to preach for a good friend of mine and I happen to turn down a random street. I see a little girl, seven or eight years old. She's so pretty but she looks so lonely. She's turning a jump rope by herself. No one is around to jump in the rope and no one is there to cheer her on. The rope is tied to a fence. I bet she has spent the entire afternoon playing jump rope with a fence. *That's no fun at all.*

I keep on driving.

At the next block, there's another little girl leaned up against a pole, eating a bag of potato chips. She looks restless. Maybe her favorite cartoons aren't on today. She crunches down on that last chip, crumples her bag into a ball, and throws her new baseball in the air. No one is around to throw the ball back and forth with her. No one is there to cheer her on. *That's no fun at all.* I drive not even two more blocks down the road. I look to the left and what do I see? Another little girl has tied her jump rope to the fence and is turning the rope by herself! *You've got to be kidding me.* I think she must've just come outside because she is turning that rope with all of her might. In a few minutes, she'll be exhausted for sure.

As I drove past these girls, I whispered to my friends in the car, "Do you realize how much fun those three girls would've had if they had just come together?"

I, TOO, HAVE A DREAM

Dear Christian Leaders,

I write this chronicle from my heart. This is my personal letter to pastors and spiritual leaders all around the world. I must confess, I am deeply saddened by what I see when I drive down a major street or a country road. There are hundreds of churches and so little transformation. There are thousands of church signs and not very much church change. I haven't been everywhere, I admit, but I have surveyed enough cities in this country to deduce that somewhere, somehow, the church has gotten distracted. One major street in Newark, NJ has over fifty churches within a three-mile radius, and the question I need answered is this: why are we turning the rope by ourselves? When are we going to come together? I see church building after church building, segregation and more segregation, denominationalism and strict separatism, and I am saddened on the one hand, and outraged on the other.

At the state the church is in, it would seem impossible to dream of a day when we can all come together. But if Dr. Martin Luther King Jr. can dare to dream, so can I. If Dr. King was brave enough to proclaim his dream to thousands of people at the Washington Monument, I can proclaim my dream to a few hundred readers. This chronicle is simply titled, "I, too, have a dream."

I have a dream that one day, Jesus will be the founder of the church again; that people will stop using egocentric terms like "my church" or "my people," and will submit to God's church and serve God's people. I have a dream that Israel will return back to her God (Hosea 14:1).[1] I have a dream that, one day, all of

God's leaders will remember that they, too, are God's followers. I have a dream that we all will finally submit to the King of Kings and dethrone the Lord of the self; that churches all over the world will look at their financial statements, count up the cost, and plan ways to bring ministries together. I have a dream today! That churches will stop looking at a mega ministries to determine their worth and mega ministries will begin to work together to establish a mightier ministry than the one she has built herself. I have a dream that the founder of the church will be Jesus Christ again.

CHURCH, IT IS TIME TO COME TOGETHER!

Psalm 133:1 Behold, how good and how pleasant it is for brethren to dwell together in unity.

Church, it is time to come together. And when I say "come together," I don't just mean annually. I don't just mean monthly. I mean, it's time for some of us to close up shop and move in with another visionary leader who shares our heart and lacks our talents. *Listen.* Every great preacher does not have to start a church. I'll say it again. Every great preacher does not have to start a church; and every great pastor does not have to be a bishop over his or her own organization! I know someone offended you, but that does not give you the right to divorce the ministry you were in! What happened to reconciliation, forgiveness, and mercy? These are the very things we can so easily preach about on Sunday, but we forget about on Monday. We apply this to personal relationships, but we forget about the church scars we've caused or the church bruises we've covered up. What are we doing? Church, it is time to come together!

If we would just open our eyes, we would repent for the way God's ministry has been man-handled. All of us. Each of us. Every single one of us needs to assess what we're doing in the name of ministry and repent for each time we assumed headship over God's church. It has become more about trophy winning than it is about soul searching. It has become about lengthy references and flashy resumes and less about self-denial and humility. If we stepped away from the mic-checks and fancy flyers, we would realize something profound. In 35 years, the church we built will need another builder. If we step back from the NOW, we will see that, indeed, time waits for no one. In just a few decades, we will have grown too old to turn the rope by ourselves. We are not going to live forever. We are not called to build mansions in tent space. We are pilgrims passing through.

I think it is interesting: We always want pastors to join our ministries, but we never think about joining someone else's. We can always envision help coming from outside of our doors, but I wonder, have you ever considered bringing your jump rope over to the next corner and telling that pastor, "Come. Let's turn this rope together?" Do you even know who the pastor is next door? Have you visited all of the churches within two miles of your own? Have you considered the force we would become if our ecclesial bases joined arms and sought God's face, acknowledging Christ as the Ultimate leader and all of us as his unnamed armour bearers?

I know you're gifted, but woe be unto the pastor who thinks he is the only mouthpiece through whom God will speak. Woe be unto the evangelist who thinks she is the only soul who can draw sinners to Christ. Woe unto the seminarian who thinks three years in school qualifies him to have Mastered Divinity. Woe to the young priest who forgets that God was speaking through deacons, mothers, and prophets long before he was born.

PARTNER? WHO, ME? YES, YOU!
COULDN'T BE…THEN WHO?

Acts 2:44-47 And all that believed were together, and had all things common; and sold their possessions and goods, and parted them to all men, as every man had need. And they, continuing daily with one accord in the temple, and breaking bread from house to house, did eat their meat with gladness and singleness of heart, praising God, and having favor with all the people. And the

Lord added to the church daily such as should be saved.

Sometimes the church is the only institution common to man that doesn't believe in partnership. Lawyers will partner, businesses and medical physicians will partner. Barbers and beauticians, pizza parlors and gas stations will partner. They realize that each practitioner has a special concentration and they are all licensed to serve in different ways, but they count up the cost and make wise business decisions. They understand that it would be cheaper to come together than it would be to pay rent, sanitation, nurses, electric, cable, internet, parking, and all other utilities by themselves. Why are we not praying for wisdom? Why are we so independent-minded and yet we call ourselves the Body of Christ? Why do we continue to see ourselves as the head of the church (or at least the neck), and not Jesus Christ? If the church came together, we could do so much more for the community. If the church came together, we could demolish our little storefronts, tight-fit tabernacles, or stadium size cathedrals, and plant a greater Christian community development center that is bigger than any University around! *Lord, help my vision to extend beyond me!* We're not thinking big enough, church! We're not thinking beyond our generation! We're wasting God's money and spoiling our resources. We're paying more bills and hosting more revivals for fundraising purposes, not for soul-winning purposes. If the church came together, our resources could actually make a difference. I know. I know. You're Lutheran. And they are Non-Denominational. And those Baptists over there, they don't like to be in church all day. I know. But, at the end of the day, please remember: doctrinal differences and denominational preferences will pass away on that great gettin' up mornin'. Our church slogan and choir chants will be of no importance in heaven. There won't be a Black Church section, a Methodist section, or a Latina evangelical section. We will all sit at the throne and join the angelic hosts in their "holy, holy, holy" mantra.

Why can't we start practicing for heaven now? Why can't we? If there won't be division in heaven, why is there division in the earth? I know there is history behind this building, but what good is a building full of history, but no *God*-story? Full of memories, and no new members. It would be an explosive revolution if the church would come together. It would grab the attention of government officials and media gurus if churches came together. And finally, God can be glorified once and for all, if the church would come together.

Consider Acts 2:44-47 for a moment. I think we can learn from the early church if we really keyed in on some important differences between them and us. First, Acts says that all of the Believers were *together*, and as a result of their togetherness, they were able to sell possessions and give to those men and women who had real needs. You see, here's our main problem. We can't give because we're too busy building. We can't build because we're too busy buying. And we can't buy because our church is still in debt! We don't sell our possessions until we get new ones. We call it giving, but we're actually just upgrading and then charging others for the stuff we no longer need. And as soon as the church gets out of the red, we start fundraising for a larger temple! What are we doing?

The second lesson I see in Acts is this: Believers all met in one temple, and they broke bread from house to house (Acts 2:46).[2] Wow! So this is how they added to the church daily. They met in one place, and they spread the word throughout their communities. That means, you can still preach, but let your dinner table become your pulpit. *Hold up.* Do your neighbors even know you're a pastor? Does the security guard in your apartment complex know that you're a Christian? What about the neighbors on the other side of your street? When is the last time you made a pulpit in your living room, and invited some friends over for a Good News day? How great would it be if we returned to the day where pastors hosted bible meetings at their houses and invited the neighborhood to dine and share in the good news of Jesus Christ? I get excited when I think about it! Do you realize how much territory we could reclaim and conquer if we would stop focusing on our little tents and actually put our resources together to build one tabernacle? One community center for children. One school for struggling and low-income students. One hospital. One Christian library. One God. No "us." In every major city. One in every major town. One in every major state. It can happen. I know it can. I believe it will! But will you believe with me? Will you tell others about it? What if God is pushing us together now because He is preparing to come back for His church? Can God be prompting us to prepare for the Second Coming and therefore, all of our territorial and earthly administrations will soon be null and void? Can you see God in the foreclosure notice your church received? Can you see God in the sudden decline in tithe and offering? No, you probably can't see Him. But you can't see Him because you don't *want* to see Him. So, instead of changing your plans and opening yourself up to a new reality in Christ Jesus, you just tax and harass people to give more to a church that may have reached its spiritual expiration date. *Ouch.*

What are we doing?

Why are we doing it?

When are we going to come together?

Is it really that bad an idea if one pastor preaches one Sunday and another pastor preaches another Sunday? *I know you have your favorites, but shouldn't our favorite voice be the voice of God? Isn't it dangerous to idolize one preacher over another preacher?* If the people can come together and the church grows as a result of it, then why can't we dare to believe that God will work out all of the fine details?

GOD, HOW DO I...AHH NEVERMIND, I'LL JUST GO TO GOOGLE.COM

James 1:5 If any of you lack wisdom, let him ask of God, that giveth to all men liberally, and upbraideth not; and it shall be given him.

I wonder if we're asking God for direction anymore, or if we're treating the church like a google.com service or an

entrepreneurial business idea. I wonder if we're being led of God
to do God's work or if people who see things in us are influencing
us more than the God who called us (Galatians 1:8).[3]   I just
wonder.   I wonder if our biggest struggle today is not lust or
greed, but impatience. We can't wait for the right season
(Ecclesiastes 3:1)[4] and so we move out before time. We can't wait
for change to happen where we are, so we relocate and join
another church, as if joining churches is the new hobby. I wonder
what would happen if we truly learned how to wait on the Lord
and hear God's voice clearly. I definitely believe that change will
come in the land and growth will happen in the church. *Just wait
on God.*

And for some of us, the issue isn't impatience; it's pride.
Every now and then we've got to swallow pride and move into the
shelter, safety and counsel of other Christian witnesses. God is
waiting for a people who aren't too prideful to admit, "I need
help," and a leader who is humble enough to say, "I don't have to
lead." Often, if we would just be honest, we hold onto ministry
names not because God said so, but because church has become
the new family business. We keep expired people in position not
because God said so, but because positions and titles are more
about promotion than they are about purpose. It's a scary day in
the halls of a man-sustained church when a popular vote trumps
God's voice. It's a scary day in the lives of a Christian when my
Sunday outfit becomes more important than my every-day
relationship with God. We get offended because the pastor said
something that we didn't like, and in a heartbeat, we leave one
church, join another, dislike the pastor there, and decide to start
our own. *Forget the anointing. I'm walking in my authority.*

What are we doing?

Why are we doing it?

When are we going to come together?

NEW PASTORS, BEWARE: TRUE MINISTRY REQUIRES WORK

Please hear my heart and do not misunderstand my speech
(John 8:43).[5] I am not downing anyone who has felt an urgency to

pastor. I honor you and applaud you for your courage. I think the call to pastor is harder than being the President of the United States. I mean, at least the President has a ghostwriter to help him write his speeches, a cabinet of qualified politicians to make decisions with him, and a host of advisors and specialists to steer him in the right direction. The call to pastoral work, on the other hand, is a lonely call. You rarely receive proper appreciation. Many people don't take your vocation seriously, and most times, church people will send you to the grave quicker than your own family if you let them!

So, if you're a pastor, I tip my hat to you. And if you endeavor to become a pastor, I tip two hats to you. But, please, please, pretty please take your call into careful consideration. *Pray. Pray again. Fast and Pray* (Matthew 17:21).[6] Think further down the line than next year. Imagine the possibility that just maybe your church will never be as big as you think it deserves to be. Ministry is hard work. People will depend on you to lead them to God. People will drain you to the point where you will want to leave church and forget God altogether. *Just tell the truth. Some of you reading aren't even pastoring and you've already wanted to leave God because of what someone else did or said to you.* Pastoring is no light burden. You won't be able to take a day off and expect the people to just pastor themselves. When you begin a ministry, it's like having a child. You can't turn around three years in and yell, "Oops. I made a mistake." No! No! No! Your "Oops" will affect many people's view about God, and the blood will be accounted to your hands for mishandling God's sheep (Ezekiel 33:6).[7]

If you sense the call to pastor, follow the call. But make sure you ask God for specific instructions as well. Not every pastor is a shepherd over a flock in the conventional sense. Not every pastor will have her or his name plastered over the top of a church sign. *I see many names on signs, but are those names written in the Book of Life* (Revelation 20:12)?[8] Some pastors are called to lead a school system into serious relationship with God. Some pastors are called to join with other pastors and use their wisdom collectively to gear God's people into a multi-layered relationship with God. Some pastors will never have a building to house their church.

Young pastors and senior bishops, ask God for fresh instructions as it relates to your particular call, and be careful not to simply assume that God will do the same for you as God did for others. Be careful not to put a "to do" list on God and require that He give you land for a building He never told you to build. It's not enough to utter words and ask for God's leading. We've got to listen to what God says even if it's not what we want to hear. We've got to open up our eyes and see the three girls on the corner street as a sign of God's disappointment. We've got to humble ourselves and be willing to serve other ministries, not for the recognition, but for the sake of God's kingdom.

------------◈------------

Jehovah God, Empty us out of any evidence that points back to our human fingerprints; so that Your glory might enlarge itself inside these earthen vessels with or without our revisions, enhancements, or second opinion.

------------◈------------

ARE YOU IN MINISTRY OR MINE-STRY?

Matthew 18:20 For where two or three are gathered together in my name, there am I in the midst of them.

Philippians 4:13 I can do all things through Christ which strengthens me.

The bible says in Matthew 18:20, "For where two or three are gathered together in my name, there am I in the midst of them." Somebody please tell me, where is God in the midst of these independent, one-man shows we call church? Many people gather, but how many people are gathering *together* in God's name? Are you serving in a ministry, or are you busy building a *mine-stry*—where it is all about you and less about Jesus? Who gets all of the attention on your website? Why are all the flyers filled with your picture? When is the last time you gave the offering back to the church? Are you in a ministry or a *mine*-stry? Is the pastor abusing the people by sending them to coal mines to get gold from the nearest ATM? Have you seen more money invested in the décor than in the local neighborhood? I just need to know: Is it about what God can do through you, or is it about what you think you can build for God? Trust me, God doesn't need your hands. He'd much rather have your heart. And, just because you *can* pastor, doesn't mean God has called you to pastor. I can take out garbage but that doesn't mean I'm called to lead janitorial services! I can sing a little bit, but does that mean I should automatically go out and audition for American Idol? No. It may be my calling, but what is my assignment? Singing publicly may be my assignment, but what are God's instructions? These are all important questions to ask before you run outside and start turning the jump rope by yourself.

*Lord, help your people. We are willing but we aren't obeying (*Isaiah 1:19).[9] *We have a zeal, but not according to knowledge* (Romans 10:2).[10] *Lord, help your people.*

Maybe God has assigned me to pastor my fellow custodian workers, and perhaps God has instructed me to work in a public school system in order to introduce Christ to someone who will never set foot in a church. Maybe I have a pastoral eye, but I also have a gift to write. Perhaps, God has instructed me to encourage a league of field-working pastors while I, myself, go to the local temple and learn from someone else. I can learn from another qualified pastor, too! That's what ministry is. It's not about me. It's all about Jesus.

Which brings me to my next point. Brothers and sisters, we've got to get delivered from this "I can do all things" mentality. We've got to understand that "I can do all things through Christ," means we can't do anything without another member in the body of Christ. Through Christ means with others in Christ. We can't do anything for God without depositing our gifts into Christ's hands first, so that He can give us out as it pleases Him (1 Corinthians 12:18).[11] This is true unity. God's idea of Unity will take our "I" knots out and untie them so that the only noticeable part of the shoelace is the Head and not the strands in between. Look at how the word is spelled. If you separate the word u-n-i-t-y, you will discover the letter "I" *not* in the beginning of the word, nor in the end of the word, but in the middle it. The "I" is surrounded by UNTY. Now call me crazy, but I even see God in this. Unity has a way of UNTYING the knot of "I did it," "I am the leader of it," and "I am the pastor over it." We don't know what unity is until we have untied our bulky knots of individuality. Anything that brings attention to our "I" needs to be crucified. Then and only then can we learn to embrace and appreciate the U's, the N's, the T's, and the Y's in our lives. I can go deeper. U-N-I-T-Y. 5 letters. 5 fingers. The middle finger is like the "I," but no hand can fully function by using the middle finger alone. So, no matter how long my middle finger is in comparison to the other members of my hand, the fact of the matter is, I need my thumb, my pinky, and everything in between in order to function properly.

The point is, we must bury our "I" in the middle of unity and always remember that even though God uses us individually, it is always for the purposes of doing greater around us, than it is in us and by us. It ain't about the "I." It's about the US. JES-US.

------------ ◈ ------------

Prayer: Lord, blend our separate strands into one beautiful shoe lace. Amen

------------ ◈ ------------

What are we doing?
Why are we doing it?
When are we going to come together?

THE BENEFITS OF COMING TOGETHER

Here are a few benefits of coming together. When you come together, you get to learn new and easier ways to do what was once hard and ineffective. When you come together, you get a chance to focus on what God has specifically called you to do instead of exhausting your time trying to do something you were never supposed to do. When you come together, you find relief in friendship and safety in counsel (Proverbs 11:14).[12] You get to see how much easier ministry is for a team than it would be for a one-woman show. When you come together, you are humbled in the presence of people who can do something better than you! You realize how much you need the other to survive. When you come together, it becomes more than a song you sing or a sermon you preach. When the church comes together, we won't get these fly by night, quickie sermons that some preachers have stolen from the Internet because they didn't have time to study.

You really can't go wrong by coming together, so why don't we give it a try? The more we rely on others and entrust the weight of ministry into others' hands, the better we are able to focus. *Be honest.* Our churches have many things, but one thing we lack…is focus.

I know. I know. Many will not hear me speaking directly to them. They'll be thinking about some other person or some other church because God has already given the name of their church and the Scripture to match. You saw a vision and there were worshippers all around you. Yes, I believe you and I also believe God. But can I remind you about Abraham and Isaac? It was God who told Abraham to sacrifice his son, and then God told him to stop and do something else (Genesis 22:1-3; Genesis 22:11-12).[13-14]

---◇---

Prayer: Lord, Move me from ark to altar. Help me not to get stuck in the floods of ministry and drown out your purpose within me. I don't want to expire inside of an ark that you no longer desire for me to be in. Amen

---◇---

Now, had Abraham memorized the instructions and stopped listening to God's voice, he would've killed his son. Can I also remind you about Noah and the ark? It was God who instructed Noah to build an ark and save his family and two of every living creature (Genesis 6:19).[15] Now, Noah built the ark, but God didn't tell Noah to live in it years after it stopped raining. There was a purpose for the ark, and there was a purpose for the altar Noah built after he left the ark (Genesis 8:20).[16] Where is the rain in your ministry? When's the last time the presence of God flooded your sanctuary? Are you in a spiritual drought and you don't even know it?

We cannot afford to get stuck on yesterday's word or yesterday's directions and forget to seek God for a fresh Word. That's the problem Jesus had with tradition (Mark 7:13).[17] Tradition becomes tradition not when you do the same thing over and over again—no that's called faithfulness; tradition becomes tradition when you make a rule out of a moment in history. Please don't make a rule out of history. Flow with God. I know you've pastored for 25 years. *Awesome. Now, do something else.* Maybe just maybe God is talking to you! Yes, you! Don't be stubborn. God is God, and there is a purpose behind every transition.

MARRIED TO MINISTRY: MASKING OUR WAY AS GOD'S WAY

I've discovered that most times, ministers stay in ministry because they are married to it, and since, in their mind, God doesn't condone divorce, they think that God doesn't honor their decision to retire or "give up." Other ministers just can't envision life without the title "Pastor" next to their name. Now listen, I too do not condone divorce, and I know it might be really hard to walk away from what you've built all of your life, but (like we say in church) if a man is hitting on you like a punching bag, you've got to go to God and get a fresh Word (after you leave the house). To me, staying in a marriage that threatens your life is not wise at all; and the same can be said for abusive ministries.

If God has joined you to a ministry, and somehow it has become abusive—the people are abused and enslaved to the church, and the leader is abused and enslaved to the church—I believe you've got to go to God and get a fresh Word. I have witnessed too many preachers who have already divorced ministry but are staying in the marriage for the kids. They put on a good show in church, but when they drive off of the church property, they argue with God like Moses did on the mountaintop (Exodus 33:11).[18] It's abusive. They are tired of being let down, they are hurting and depressed, they feel used, and they often find themselves wondering if God ever meant for them to go through so much pain. Alone. They feel guilty and obligated. They feel like a recycle bin full of clear bottles and used paper. They get up and encourage you to fight on, but they quickly end up forfeiting after the audience goes to sleep. They give all of themselves every single day for the greater good, and they go home empty.

Lord, flush out our gloomy images of ministry and give us a new blueprint. Grant more ministerial opportunities in the world in which we live, and not just the church we haphazardly attend.

Let me share something with you, my dear sister or brother—wherever you may be. First things first: you have *not* let God down. In fact, you haven't failed at anything yet. But if you continue down this road, you may injure the innocent passengers riding with you. *Take the high road and surrender your ministry to God.* Maybe this is another confirming sign. Maybe God has been pleased with your willingness and your obedience, and now, as a reward for all of your hard labor, God will begin a new chapter in your life. I don't know, but I do believe that you're reading this for a reason; and if you would simply accept what God has willed, I guarantee you, your release will free you to finish the work you keep putting off.

THE BURDEN OF DOING MINISTRY ALONE

There comes a time in every minister's life that he or she must stop, look around, and ask two questions: "What am I doing?" and "Have I lost focus of the purpose of this ministry?"

What the people yearn for can distract us. *People can take you off course if you let them.* The church next door can discourage us. *The lust of the eye will glare at more than beautiful bodies and lovely faces.* If we are not careful, we will start to compare ourselves to other ministries. Pretty soon, if we leave this attitude untamed, it will breed a spirit of competition and an "I don't need nobody else" mentality. But that is one of the biggest lies we've ever told. *I don't need nobody else.* The Bible doesn't support this declaration of independence, and neither do life circumstances. Nehemiah needed people to help build the wall (Nehemiah 4:6).[19] Moses had Aaron and an army of elders to help organize the children of Israel (Exodus 12:21).[20] Adam was given Eve (Genesis 1:28).[21] Paul was given Silas (Acts 16:25).[22] Jesus chose twelve disciples (Luke 6:13),[23] and Paul wrote about the five-fold ministry to highlight the importance of a diversity of gifts in the church (Ephesians 4:11-13).[24] God appointed leaders for a purpose, absolutely, but He never left leaders without help and a team. I don't believe God intended for the burden of ministry to fall on the shoulders of one person. If you're a human being who does anything in the world, you're going to need somebody else at some point. We spend years and years doing ministry by ourselves. It's time to come together. People are living in a day of financial deficit. The church is not exempt. We need a plan of action and we need a plan now. Before we open the doors of another church, I think we should pray and ask God how we might use our rope, and another's rope, so that we can combine forces and make ministry happen in a more excellent way.

I pray this chronicle will create a ricochet effect in the world. I pray that people will stop building ministries with their own hands and will begin to put the vision and purpose of God's church back into the nail-scarred hands of Jesus Christ. It is in Him that we live, we move, and we have our being (Acts 17:28).[25] His hands did the hard work so that our manicured fingernails could rest in the Finished work of Jesus Christ. Let's come together. Let's work together. Let's end this separateness and division, and let's dare to believe that God can. I believe God can and God will do exceeding and abundant things once we stop turning the rope by ourselves. It will be uncomfortable at first, but in the end, it will be worth it. It will cause us to stretch, but God will be pleased. I know it seems impossible, but I serve a God who specializes in the impossible. I have no doubt. God will do the impossible…if we just believe. *I, too, have a dream.*

Ephesians 4:1-6

I therefore, the prisoner of the Lord, beseech you that ye walk worthy of the vocation wherewith ye are called, with all lowliness and meekness, with long-suffering, forbearing one another in love; endeavoring to keep the unity of the Spirit in the bond of peace. There is one body, and one Spirit, even as ye are called in one hope of your calling; one Lord, one faith, one baptism, one God and Father of all, who is above all, and through all, and in you all.

------------ ◈ ------------

Heavenly Chief, I've learned that doing ministry Your way requires more than a good speaker and an expensive microphone. It requires obedience, sacrifice, and selflessness. Help me to obey, help me to sacrifice, and help me to serve. In Christ's name, Amen.

------------ ◈ ------------

Questions for Introspection

☙_____❧

1) How can you make this dream become a reality? With whom can you share this chronicle?

2) Look through your phonebook. Does everyone in your phonebook know that you are Christian? Yes? Great! If "yes", then call about five people and invite them to turn the rope with you. If "no," then how about you invite someone to church this Sunday. *Believe me.* Some little girl out there needs your help!

Practical Points

1 The question we should all be asking is, "Which ministry does this better than me and how can I serve that ministry?" This question should not be confused with, "You come to my church and give fifty dollars and I come to your church and give $35." No. The church of tomorrow is that church interested in bridging different groups of people together, contributing to the local church, and adding depth to the global church.

2 Never limit God. Maybe you don't have to start ministry from scratch. Maybe there is a church out there waiting for a pastor like you to come in and assist them. Think about it. Pray about it. Before you build a new house, make sure there are no "houses for sale." And if you are so caught up in trying to build your own house, make sure it's not because you feel the need to have your signature on God's church.

3 Look at ministry like a relay race and then you'll learn how to depend on others to win the prize. Someone in the body of Christ needs your help. Reach out for the baton. Turn the rope for someone else.

4 Had Abraham memorized the instructions and stopped listening to God's voice, he would've killed his son. Listen to the voice of God and turn down the voice of doubt. When it's time to make a pivotal move in God, you'll know. Everywhere you go, there will be signs pointing toward the open door. Follow God even if it's humiliating and costly. It usually is anyway.

5 When nations get in crisis mode, they do things together that they would've never thought to do under regular circumstances. Republicans and Democrats come together. Whole families move in with each other when a crisis knocks on the door. Church, look around! We are in a crisis. God is pulling us together so that we can revive our nation and prepare for Christ's soon return.

Scripture Glossary

ᚲ⧽_____⧽ᚲ

[1]**Hosea 14:1** *O israel, return unto the LORD thy God; for thou hast fallen by thine iniquity.*

[2]**Acts 2:46** *And they, continuing daily with one accord in the temple, and breaking bread from house to house, did eat their meat with gladness and singleness of heart.*

[3]**Galatians 1:8** *But though we, or an angel from heaven, preach any other gospel unto you than that which we have preached unto you, let him be accursed.*

[4]**Ecclesiastes 3:1** *To every thing there is a season, and a time to every purpose under the heaven.*

[5]**John 8:43** *Why do ye not understand my speech? even because ye cannot hear my word.*

[6]**Matthew 17:21** *Howbeit this kind goeth not out but by prayer and fasting.*

[7]**Ezekiel 33:6** *But if the watchman see the sword come, and blow*

not the trumpet, and the people be not warned; if the sword come, and take any person from among them, he is taken away in his iniquity; but his blood will I require at the watchman's hand.

[8]**Revelation 20:12** *And I saw the dead, small and great, stand before God; and the books were opened: and another book was opened, which is the book of life: and the dead were judged out of those things which were written in the books, according to their works.*

[9]**Isaiah 1:19** *If ye be willing and obedient, ye shall eat the good of the land.*

[10]**Romans 10:2** *For I bear them record that they have a zeal of God, but not according to knowledge.*

[11]**1 Corinthians 12:18** *But now hath God set the members every one of them in the body, as it hath pleased him.*

[12]**Proverbs 11:14** *Where no counsel is, the people fall: but in the multitude of counsellors there is safety.*

[13]**Genesis 22:1-3** *And it came to pass after these things, that God did tempt Abraham, and said unto him, Abraham: and he said, Behold, here I am. And he said, Take now thy son, thine only son Isaac, whom thou lovest, and get thee into the land of Moriah; and offer him there for a burnt offering upon one of the mountains which I will tell thee of. And Abraham rose up early in the morning, and saddled his ass, and took two of his young men with him, and Isaac his son, and clave the wood for the burnt offering, and rose up, and went unto the place of which God had told him.*

[14]**Genesis 22:11-12** *And the angel of the LORD called unto him out of heaven, and said, Abraham, Abraham: and he said, Here am I. And he said, Lay not thine hand upon the lad, neither do thou any*

thing unto him: for now I know that thou fearest God, seeing thou hast not withheld thy son, thine only son from me.

[15]**Genesis 6:19** *And of every living thing of all flesh, two of every sort shalt thou bring into the ark, to keep them alive with thee; they shall be male and female.*

[16]**Genesis 8:20** *And Noah builded an altar unto the LORD; and took of every clean beast, and of every clean fowl, and offered burnt offerings on the altar.*

[17]**Mark 7:13** *Making the word of God of none effect through your tradition, which ye have delivered: and many such like things do ye.*

[18]**Exodus 33:11** *And the LORD spake unto Moses face to face, as a man speaketh unto his friend. And he turned again into the camp: but his servant Joshua, the son of Nun, a young man, departed not out of the tabernacle.*

[19]**Nehemiah 4:6** *So built we the wall; and all the wall was joined together unto the half thereof: for the people had a mind to work.*

[20]**Exodus 12:21** *Then Moses called for all the elders of Israel, and said unto them, Draw out and take you a lamb according to your families, and kill the passover.*

[21]**Genesis 1:28** *And God blessed them, and God said unto them, Be fruitful, and multiply, and replenish the earth, and subdue it: and have dominion over the fish of the sea, and over the fowl of the air, and over every living thing that moveth upon the earth.*

[22]**Acts 16:25** *And at midnight Paul and Silas prayed, and sang praises unto God: and the prisoners heard them.*

23**Luke 6:13** *And when it was day, he called unto him his disciples: and of them he chose twelve, whom also he named apostles.*

24**Ephesians 4:11-13** *And he gave some, apostles; and some, prophets; and some, evangelists; and some, pastors and teachers; For the perfecting of the saints, for the work of the ministry, for the edifying of the body of Christ: Till we all come in the unity of the faith, and of the knowledge of the Son of God, unto a perfect man, unto the measure of the stature of the fulness of Christ.*

25**Acts 17:28** *For in him we live, and move, and have our being; as certain also of your own poets have said, For we are also his offspring.*

CHRONICLES THAT *EVANGELIZE*

ೞ_____ೞ

WITNESSING THE DEATH OF A SQUIRREL

What does Salvation mean to me?

ભ_____ ૭

For all have sinned, and come short of the glory of God;
Romans 3:23

And this is the will of him that sent me, that every one which seeth the Son, and believeth on him, may have everlasting life: and I will raise him up at the last day.
John 6:40

For the wages of sin is death; but the gift of God is eternal life through Jesus Christ our Lord.
Romans 6:23

"Salvation is an open-book exam; maybe that's why so many people fail. God filled in the answer sheet before He administered the exam—so why is Hell so full?"
—Lawrence Alexander

$\mathcal{D}$riving down the road toward Interstate 280 in NJ. I'm rushing somewhere. *I'm always rushing.* It's a parade out here after 2:00pm. Crossing guards are whistling and children are screaming. Kids are just getting out of school, and some folks are returning to work after a late lunch. All of a sudden, I hear a loud screeching noise and a little girl screams. There was no one in the road. No one seemed hurt. What was all the screaming about? *I drive ahead.* The cars in front of me shift into the other lane and bend around something in the road. I can't see it from where I am. "Must be a pothole," I thought. "No big deal."

I inch up a few car lengths ahead, and lo and behold, an injured squirrel is fighting to keep his life in the middle of the road. Now, if you know me, you know that I really don't like rodents, much less staring at an injured rodent while driving. But, there was something about this squirrel that drew me in. There was something about the way he squirmed his little tail anxiously, convulsing in the street like a shaken up soda can that choked me up a little bit. I felt bad for him. He had been hit by a car; hit by another distracted someone who was rushing along his or her merry way like I was that day. But, the squirrel didn't die. He was half dead, yes, but he was still alive. Wriggling around like a worm, yes, but he was still alive. He was created to move quickly, and now someone's car had destroyed the nature of this squirrel's life…maybe for the rest of his life, but he was still alive. No one helped the squirrel get out of the middle of the street. I mean, it was a squirrel. Who touches those? I passed around this quivering squirrel and thought to myself, "If someone doesn't move quickly, he'll just get hit again and die." Yet, I did nothing to save his life. I saw the problem. I predicted the future, but I did nothing to change it. *Sounds like so many other Christians I know.*

I don't know what happened to Mr. Squirrel, but his life changed my perspective about salvation

------------ ◈ ------------

Lord, help me not to briskly pass by those who are injured, lifeless and crying out for a helping hand. Help me not to forget that outside of the biggest church could be a begging angel waiting for me to tend to her needs. Please help me not to forget. Amen

------------ ◈ ------------

forever. I sped along, but I couldn't stop thinking about how many people we leave out in the middle of the road. We don't want to touch "those" kinds of folk. We blame people for jumping out and getting in our way, when the truth is, it is more the fault of the driver who was not paying attention than it was the squirrel who was innocently doing what he's always done. The squirrels we ignore everyday need a Savior, too. Of course, I'm not talking about the rodent. I'm talking about the hitchhiker that we label as road kill, or the homeless man at the traffic light whom we barely see. The squirrels of our society need a Savior, too. Everyone needs to know Jesus. And yet, we drive along, on our way to church, and pass right by God.

Hebrews 13:2 Be not forgetful to entertain strangers: for thereby some have entertained angels unawares.

WE ARE HUMAN, WE HAVE SINNED, BUT JESUS SAVED THE DAY

This chronicle is dedicated to all of the "squirrels" that may be lying in the middle of the road. I want to try and explain to you what salvation is (in my own creative way) and then I want to extend the opportunity for you to know Christ. I'll begin by saying this:

If salvation had a price tag, we could never afford it.
If perfection was a bad habit, we could never support it.
If heaven had auditions, I would never make the cast.
If I applied for salvation, my application would be denied.

It is so important to understand *why* we need to be "saved." Why should I receive salvation? Why do I even need salvation? Answer: Because we all have sinned (Romans 3:23).[1] The word "sin," simply defined, means to miss the mark, and all of us, at one point, have aimed at the bull's eye of perfection and missed the mark. If we didn't, we wouldn't be human. We all entered the world with the inclination to misbehave (Psalm 51:5).[2] If you didn't steal cookies from the cookie jar, you snuck to watch television after bedtime, or you forged your mom's signature to get out of a parent/teacher conference. The older we grew, the more daring we became. We may not have murdered someone or stolen from a bank, but we probably embellished a little on our income tax reports, text-messaged a friend while driving, or perhaps cheated on a spouse. There is no big or little sin. It's all frowned upon in God's eyes and every one of these examples serve as sufficient evidence to prove one minor glitch about humans—we enjoy doing things we're not supposed to do. Like the highlighted Scripture above states, "We all have sinned and come short of the glory of God." And I've got news for you. All means all. As beautiful as we are, we all have sinned. As lucrative as our family business is, we all have sinned. Despite the degrees and the decrees, we all have sinned. Sin is humanity's maiden name and the only way to change our name is to marry Christ.

We could never value the assets of salvation until we realize the liabilities of sin. If you don't understand the penalty of sin, you'll certainly never understand the purpose behind Christ's hospital visit to Earth. Here's a quick historical review. From the fall of Adam until the birth of Immanuel (God with us), God's creation grew sicker by the generation. Various covenants, prophets, and kings were established to bring humanity out of their slum, but unfortunately, all the king's horses and all the king's men, couldn't put Humpty back together again. Abraham tried, but failed. Noah tried, but failed. David tried, but failed. Why? Because like us, they were human squirrels too, standing in the need of a Savior. Sin overwhelmed us to the point of death and destruction was the only option for mankind. We were headed to hell, but God intervened.

God never desired that we perish (2 Peter 3:9),[3] so He assumed His role as Lifeguard and dove into the polluted waters of Earth to rescue creation Himself. God brought heaven to earth through His only begotten Son, Jesus Christ. Jesus lived on Earth to prove who God was (Matthew 22:32),[4] He died on the cross to prove who God is (John 2:19),[5] and Jesus rose from the grave to prove who God will always be (John 11:25).[6] Christ's death, burial and resurrection functioned as the perfect salvation plan necessary to conquer and overtake the undefeated Goliath of sin. When Jesus died, we were completely set free. When Jesus rose, we were fully redeemed(1 Peter 1:18-19).[7] When Jesus returned to heaven, we were empowered by His Spirit (John 14:26).[8] Think about it. He did all of that for us. Who wouldn't want to serve a God like this?

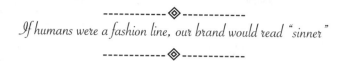

------------ ◈ ------------
If humans were a fashion line, our brand would read "sinner"
------------ ◈ ------------

DEFINING SALVATION: A PARABLE TO MAKE SALVATION CLEAR

Now that we've answered the "why" question, let's consider this question for a moment: "what is salvation?" I'll use another analogy. Let's imagine that all of us are preparing a wonderful dinner for our respective family. So, the first thing we need is a pot, right? Right. And where are pots stored? Well, in most kitchens, pots are stored in dark cabinet spaces, right? Right. *But, we have an issue.* In order for a pot to be used for its primary purpose, the cook must reach inside of the dark and cozy cabinet, pull the pot out from among its neighborhood, and clean accordingly. Now, stay with me because I'm going somewhere (*I love when preachers say that!)*— cleaning is essential. Why? Because no one wants to eat from anything that is dirty! So, there are three things that every cook (in compliance with the sanitation department) needs to do before any cooking takes place: we rinse, we remove, and we refill.

1) We rinse the pot.
2) We remove the dirty contents out into the sink.
3) We refill the empty pot in preparation for boiling.

We use one resource to do three things: the water. But how do we get the water? Oh, well nowadays, we go to a faucet. *Faucet.* Yes, thanks to Al Moen's invention of the water faucet in 1937, all cooks have access to the water supply through a small valve called the faucet. This faucet controls the flow of water, and it is also used to extract the water. Why do we need a faucet you ask? Because quite frankly, life would be too difficult without it.

Here's the fun part. We serve Jesus, because quite frankly, life would be too difficult without Him. Jesus is the cook, the faucet, the water, and the sink. It was Jesus who pulled us out from the cabinet of sin, it is Jesus who washed us (and continues to wash us) thoroughly with His fresh waters (Psalm 51:2).[9] And it is Jesus who obligated Himself to exchange our filthy sins with His life, so that we could obtain eternal life. He is the sink of our salvation because He dumped all of our sins onto Himself, carried them to the cross, and died. He is the faucet of our faith, because in Him contained all that we needed to receive forgiveness from and atonement for our sins (Acts 26:18).[10]

> *We all were dirty once, but after we embraced salvation, the waters of His Spirit filled our empty pot with purpose, joy, satisfaction, and an abundance of other spiritual remedies that all in all, make life worth living.*

As His blood spewed out on the climax of human history (Crucifixion day), the world received a gazillion salvation babies (Hebrews 9:22).[11] The contents inside of the faucet—in this case water and blood (John 19:34)[12]— exploded out onto all of humanity, including generations unborn and pre-born. This explosion, without a doubt, reformed our worship experience, brought us closer to the Father in heaven, and repaired the damage that we had done (2 Corinthians 5:18).[13] While we were yet sinners, Christ died (Romans 5:8).[14] While we were half-dead, in the middle of the road, He died. While we were snoring, Christ was cooking breakfast for his children. Christ strategically mapped out our rescue boats from the slum of sin, and then He sank so that we could swim.

HOW ARE WE SAVED?

Ephesians 2:8 For by grace are ye saved through faith; and that not of yourselves: it is the gift of God:

Grace. There's no way I can talk about salvation, sin, rescue, recovery, and all of the above without underlining the most important word in my salvation dictionary. *Grace.* Everything I've said, and everything I've written (in this chronicle and every chronicle preceding this one) can only be spoken about because of grace. We are not saved as a result of our good deeds. We are not even saved because we deserve to be saved. Rather, we are saved by grace through faith. In other words, we are saved because God stepped out as a Holy Conductor before us, provided the instruments we would need to participate in His orchestra, and then God stood back and waited for us to pick up the instrument and play for His glory. So what is grace? How can I explain this marvelous gift to everyone? Well, for starters, you can think about the four ways we use the word 'grace' in everyday life. Think about it. We use grace to describe someone's beauty or elegance, right? Right. So, if Cinderella were to walk into a ballroom, most of us would say something like, "She looks so graceful;" and heavenly grace is no different. Grace is God's beauty over me. Grace is God's outstanding loveliness tailor-made for me. In grace, His elegance outshines my ugliness and because of grace, His blood conceals my stains. That's grace.

Grace is also something we ask people to say before we eat our food. "Don't forget to say your grace!" we exclaim right before we chomp down into that tasty cheeseburger. Well, heavenly grace is no different. God blessed my food before I sat down at the table. That's grace. Grace is God's prayer of blessing over me before others took part of my broken bread. That's grace.

Grace is a word we use in exchange for a favor. Even church people love to define grace as the "favor of God." But do we think about this in simple yet profound ways, too? If we did, I think we would recognize something magnificent. Think about it. In grace, God did me a favor without me ever asking for it. He foreknew that I would need a bail out plan far bigger than any stimulus package or health care reform could imitate, and so, by grace, God saved me from the world before He shipped me into it. God conceived of a salvation plan in His mind before Adam and Eve were deceived in their hearts. That's grace. Grace is God's heavenly acceptance letter to us before my resignation letter to the world. That's a heavenly favor. But not the kind of favor that gets us a car with bad credit. No, that's more like cheap luck I think. God gives everlasting favor and He never plans on asking us to pay Him back.

But, that's not all! There's another way to define grace. *Grace Period.* You know how we usually give people a grace period if they have missed a deadline or returned a library book after its expiration date? Yes, this is also a great way to comprehend another aspect of grace to those who need more of it. *God knows I need as much grace as I can find!* Check this out. God not only awarded me with life, but God calculated my pit stops and didn't stop loving me. God gave me time to catch up and didn't charge me for paying my bills late. God never kicked me out of class for coming in tardy. In fact, God let me graduate even if I didn't ace all of my classes, because it was never about me getting an A in the first place. This is grace. He didn't sue me for being a sinner. Instead, He assumed my debt, died for every sin I deposited into my fleshly bank account, and favored me with a million second chances per year. Oh yes, I'm a millionaire. A grace-receiving millionaire. A grace recipient who showed up late and God said, "Right on time!" Yes, this is grace.

So ask me how I'm saved? And I'll tell you "by grace am I saved through faith." Not because I'm great, but because of God's grace. Not because my faith in God is great, but more exactly, because God's faith in me is greater.

SALVATION IS THROUGH JESUS AND JESUS ALONE

John 14:6 Jesus saith unto him, I am the way, the truth, and the life: no man cometh unto the Father, but by me.

Mark 13:13 And you shall be hated of all men for my name's sake: but he that shall endure to the end, the same shall be saved.

So we've answered the *why*, *what*, and *how* questions about salvation. But now I want to reiterate, (this is very important) the *who* and only *who* question. Then, I'll end with a prayer for those who desire to know Christ personally. Know this: through Jesus Christ we are saved. Jesus is the *Who,* the perfect sacrifice (Hebrews 9:11-16),[15] our heavenly intercessor (Romans 8:34),[16] and our Risen King (1 Corinthians 15:2).[17] Jesus is the bridge that connects you to eternal life/heaven (John 14:6).[18] God gave His *only* Son from eternity's emergency room, "so that whosoever would believe on Him, would not perish, but would have everlasting life" (John 3:16).[19] Jesus Christ clothed himself in a faucet of human flesh, exported the Holy Water from heaven to earth, and His death, burial and resurrection dispensed all of the elements we needed to be rinsed, removed and refilled. So the next time you pick up a pot in your kitchen, just tell the Lord, "Thank you for pulling me out, washing me through and through, and filling me with your precious Spirit." Because of Jesus, we are. We are able to live a guilt-free life. We are able to walk in God's abundance, strength, and knowledge. What a privilege it is to know Christ and to be known by Him!

For the reader who hasn't received Jesus Christ as Lord and Savior, many people teach that all you have to do is repent, confess, believe, and go to church. And yes, repentance is necessary (Acts 2:38),[20] confession is crucial (Romans 10:9-10),[21] belief in God is primary (Hebrews 11:6; Mark 16:16),[22-23] and community is strongly encouraged (Hebrews 10:25).[24] But, one small detail must be clarified. Coming to Jesus does not mean you will never have another issue in your life. In fact, coming to Jesus might mean you'll face more opposition, more misunderstanding, or even betrayal. But be of good cheer! If the world hates you, know that it hated Christ before it hated you (John 15:18).[25] Scripture also states, "Think it not strange concerning the fiery trial which is to try you as though some strange thing happened to you" (1 Peter 4:12).[26] I don't want you to be deceived. Salvation is not like waving a magic wand in front of you and erasing all trials from your life. No. In fact, life brings trials—that's just a part of life—but when you accept Christ, you receive help. You receive strength. You receive wisdom and accountability. Your trials have purpose and God's promises are sure and lasting. Knowing Christ comes with a full-time warranty of power, love, and protection. God will empower you to be victorious in every trial you face, God will love you in spite of you, and God will protect you by introducing you to His perfect will for your life. His power, His love, and His protection will change you, but it will be the best change your life could ever undergo.

When you understand that life is better with Jesus than it is without Him, and you confess that Jesus is truly the Lord over your life, repentance will become a natural reflex. When you repent, you apologize to God and turn away from the dark cabinet of sin and emptiness (Acts 3:19).[27] You become a "Christian" by accepting that salvation baby and nurturing the gift that Jesus Christ has freely given to you (Philippians 2:12).[28]

WHY DO I NEED TO KNOW JESUS?

Revelation 3:20 Behold, I stand at the door, and knock: if any man hear my voice, and open the door, I will come in to him, and will sup with him, and he with me.

John 6:40 And this is the will of him that sent me, that every one which seeth the Son, and believeth on him, may have everlasting life: and I will raise him up at the last day.

The purpose for welcoming the Lord into your life is so that He can direct your steps toward heaven (John 3:16-17).[29] To not know Jesus is to starve your soul from the most rewarding gift life has to offer. To not know Jesus is to not know why you exist. But, to know Jesus is to find fulfillment and complete satisfaction in Him. To know Jesus is to meet life's greatest Life-Partner, and to become a better woman or man as a result of it. Not just better, but wiser. Not just wiser, but more caring and loving. Not just more caring and loving, but more selfless and more forgiving. To know Jesus is to...I don't know...I can't really explain it. You've just got to try Him for yourself. I pray you will. I pray you will accept Jesus today and always. Don't squabble around in the middle of the road. You have so much purpose to fulfill. God can make you whole again.

Will you accept Christ today?

If you want God in your life, all you have to do is pray and ask Him to come into your heart. Ask Him to wash you, forgive you, and cleanse you. Tell the Lord whatever you want to tell Him, and focus in on God's love. Once you do, you will begin to feel the presence of God's warm embrace.

In the space below, you can write your own prayer of salvation. I don't believe salvation is about a formula. Romans 10:13 says, "whosoever shall call upon the name of the lord shall be saved." So, call Him! There's no wrong way to scream for help if you're drowning in the ocean. Just make sure you get the Lifeguard's attention. Go ahead, write your own love letter to God and seal it with an "I believe…" (John 11:25)[30]

_____

_____

_____

_____

_____

_____

_____

_____

_____

_____

_____

_____

_____

_____

_____

_____

_____

_____

------------ ◈ ------------

Can't find the right words to say? Repeat these words: Jesus, I am a sinner and I need Your saving power. Please forgive me and come into my heart. Take my life. Rearrange me. Take my mind. Transform me. Plant within me a desire to please You. I believe you died for my sins, I believe you were buried for my sake, and I believe you rose with all power on the third day. I believe! Amen

------------ ◈ ------------

If you've accepted Jesus Christ as your Lord and Savior, let me be the first to congratulate you and remind you of what just happened. You have escaped the chokehold of sin abuse and walked into the arms of a loving God for recovery and rescue (Galatians 5:1).[31] You have freely exchanged the punishment of hell and death with the prosperity of heaven and life in Jesus Christ. You are no longer enslaved to sin (Romans 6:6-7),[32] no longer condemned by sin (Romans 8:1),[33] and no longer bound by your own limitations (John 14:12).[34] You are free in Jesus! Hallelujah! The angels in heaven are rejoicing right now (Luke 15:10)[35] because another part of God's creation has acknowledged its Creator. And trust me, I am rejoicing, too! I may never meet you or know your name, but I am still rejoicing with you. You are my sister in Christ or my brother in Christ, and I want you to know that I love you. We love you! But most of all, God loves you!

Please email us at gpi@godzchildproductions.net and let us know who you are. We'll send you a personal Bible, some information pamphlets, and we'll try our very best to connect you with another Christian community near you. Please reach out to someone. Community is key. If you are able to attend a Bible-living and Bible-teaching church, do so. If not, try to study the Word of God on a consistent basis and ask the Holy Spirit to lead you to someone who can help you to better understand His Word. God will do it. I know He will!

------------ ◈ ------------

Heavenly Father, I am praying now for the person reading this chronicle. I pray that You will flood them with the waters of Your presence. Overwhelm them with the evidence of Your warm embrace. Let the reader's life be forever changed by the power of Your hand and by the love of Your heart. Use this reader for Your glory. Use this individual to do great things for Your Kingdom. Amen.

------------ ◈ ------------

Practical Points

1 Humans have accomplished a lot, but there is one achievement that no man save Jesus Christ has earned—no other human can say they have obtained a degree in perfect living. Don't try to be a perfect being. You'll never accomplish that long-term goal. Instead, find perfection in Christ and pattern your life after Him more and more each day (Matthew 5:48).[36]

2 Like magnets on the table of life, both sin and salvation pull us closer to Jesus. By our sinful nature alone, we don't have what it takes to get into heaven. If you don't fully understand both salvation and its relationship to sin, you'll think you can make it to heaven on your own good works and deeds. You'll forget about God's grace gift to humanity and fail to benefit from the blessings that grace has afforded us.

3 He is the Potter, I am the clay. You are not the cook. You are the pot. Just a pot. I heard TD Jakes say in a sermon, "You didn't find God. God wasn't lost. Rather, God found you." That's a nice way to put it. Like the master chef in our beautiful story, God reached into the dark world of sin, exposed you to the Light, and saved your life so that you could be used by Him and for Him.

4 Salvation comes coupled with separation -- When you are saved, you are automatically separated from old things. You become new (2 Corinthians 5:17).[37] You transition from darkness to light and you find yourself yearning to be more like God.

5 The last thing an unbeliever needs to witness is a judgmental Christian. As you bask in the abundance of God's life on earth, be careful not to judge others who haven't yet come into the knowledge of Christ. *All* means all. Have patience with others because someone had patience with you. Hey, you may be the only Jesus they'll ever see.

Scripture Glossary

[1]**Romans 3:23** *For all have sinned, and come short of the glory of God.*

[2]**Psalm 51:5** *Behold, I was shapen in iniquity; and in sin did my mother conceive me.*

[3]**2 Peter 3:9** *The Lord is not slack concerning his promise, as some men count slackness; but is longsuffering to us-ward, not willing that any should perish, but that all should come to repentance.*

[4]**Matthew 22:32** *I am the God of Abraham, and the God of Isaac, and the God of Jacob? God is not the God of the dead, but of the living.*

[5]**John 2:19** *Jesus answered and said unto them, Destroy this temple, and in three days I will raise it up.*

[6]**John 11:25** *Jesus said unto her, I am the resurrection, and the life: he that believeth in me, though he were dead, yet shall he live.*

[7]**1 Peter 1:18-19** *Forasmuch as ye know that ye were not redeemed with corruptible things, as silver and gold, from your vain conversation received by tradition from your fathers; But with the precious blood of Christ, as of a lamb without blemish and without spot.*

[8]**John 14:26** *But the Comforter, which is the Holy Ghost, whom the Father will send in my name, he shall teach you all things, and bring all things to your remembrance, whatsoever I have said unto you.*

[9]**Psalm 51:2** *Wash me thoroughly from mine iniquity, and cleanse me from my sin.*

[10]**Acts 26:18** *To open their eyes, and to turn them from darkness to light, and from the power of Satan unto God, that they may receive forgiveness of sins, and inheritance among them which are sanctified by faith that is in me.*

[11]**Hebrews 9:22** *And almost all things are by the law purged with blood; and without shedding of blood is no remission.*

[12]**John 19:34** *But one of the soldiers with a spear pierced his side, and forthwith came there out blood and water.*

[13]**2 Corinthians 5:18** *And all things are of God, who hath reconciled us to himself by Jesus Christ, and hath given to us the ministry of reconciliation.*

[14]**Romans 5:8** *But God commendeth his love toward us, in that, while we were yet sinners, Christ died for us.*

[15]**Hebrews 9:11-16** *But Christ being come an high priest of good things to come, by a greater and more perfect tabernacle, not made with hands, that is to say, not of this building; Neither by the blood of goats and calves, but by his own blood he entered in once into the holy place, having obtained eternal redemption for us. For if the blood of bulls and of goats, and the ashes of an heifer sprinkling the unclean, sanctifieth to the purifying of the flesh: How much more*

shall the blood of Christ, who through the eternal Spirit offered himself without spot to God, purge your conscience from dead works to serve the living God? And for this cause he is the mediator of the new testament, that by means of death, for the redemption of the transgressions that were under the first testament, they which are called might receive the promise of eternal inheritance. For where a testament is, there must also of necessity be the death of the testator.

16**Romans 8:34** *Who is he that condemneth? It is Christ that died, yea rather, that is risen again, who is even at the right hand of God, who also maketh intercession for us.*

17**1 Corinthians 15:2** *By which also ye are saved, if ye keep in memory what I preached unto you, unless ye have believed in vain.*

18**John 14:6** *Jesus saith unto him, I am the way, the truth, and the life: no man cometh unto the Father, but by me.*

19**John 3:16** *For God so loved the world, that he gave his only begotten Son, that whosoever believeth in him should not perish, but have everlasting life.*

20**Acts 2:38** *Then Peter said unto them, Repent, and be baptized every one of you in the name of Jesus Christ for the remission of sins, and ye shall receive the gift of the Holy Ghost.*

21**Romans 10:9-10** *That if thou shalt confess with thy mouth the Lord Jesus, and shalt believe in thine heart that God hath raised him from the dead, thou shalt be saved.For with the heart man believeth unto righteousness; and with the mouth confession is made unto salvation.*

22**Hebrews 11:6** *But without faith it is impossible to please him: for he that cometh to God must believe that he is, and that he is a rewarder of them that diligently seek him.*

23**Mark 16:16** *He that believeth and is baptized shall be saved; but* *he that believeth not shall be damned.*

[24]**Hebrews 10:25** *Not forsaking the assembling of ourselves together, as the manner of some is; but exhorting one another: and so much the more, as ye see the day approaching.*

[25]**John 15:18** *If the world hate you, ye know that it hated me before it hated you.*

[26]**1 Peter 4:12** *Beloved, think it not strange concerning the fiery trial which is to try you, as though some strange thing happened unto you.*

[27]**Acts 3:19** *Repent ye therefore, and be converted, that your sins may be blotted out, when the times of refreshing shall come from the presence of the Lord.*

[28]**Philippians 2:12** *Wherefore, my beloved, as ye have always obeyed, not as in my presence only, but now much more in my absence, work out your own salvation with fear and trembling.*

[29]**John 3:16-17** *For God so loved the world, that he gave his only begotten Son, that whosoever believeth in him should not perish, but have everlasting life. For God sent not his Son into the world to condemn the world; but that the world through him might be saved.*

[30]**John 11:25** *Jesus said unto her, I am the resurrection, and the life: he that believeth in me, though he were dead, yet shall he live.*

[31]**Galatians 5:1** *Stand fast therefore in the liberty wherewith Christ hath made us free, and be not entangled again with the yoke of bondage.*

[32]**Romans 6:6-7** *Knowing this, that our old man is crucified with him, that the body of sin might be destroyed, that henceforth we should not serve sin. For he that is dead is freed from sin.*

[33]**Romans 8:1** *There is therefore now no condemnation to them which are in Christ Jesus, who walk not after the flesh, but after the Spirit.*

[34]**John 14:12** *Verily, verily, I say unto you, He that believeth on me, the works that I do shall he do also; and greater works than these shall he do; because I go unto my Father.*

[35]**Luke 15:10** *Likewise, I say unto you, there is joy in the presence of the angels of God over one sinner that repenteth.*

[36]**Matthew 5:48** *Be ye therefore perfect, even as your Father which is in heaven is perfect.*

[37]**2 Corinthians 5:17** *Therefore if any man be in Christ, he is a new creature: old things are passed away; behold, all things are become new.*

BUYING A VALENTINE'S DAY CARD

Will you be My Valentine?

℃_____℅

For God so loved the world, that he gave his only begotten Son, that whosoever believeth in him should not perish, but have everlasting life. For God sent not his Son into the world to condemn the world; but that the world through him might be saved.
John 3:16-17

Hereby perceive we the love of God, because he laid down his life for us: and we ought to lay down our lives for the brethren.
1 John 3:16

*V*alentine's Day. It can be the best of times or the worst of times. It all depends on whether you are madly in love or solemnly single. Valentine's Day. You know, February 14th. It's a night when babies are conceived and a day when the deepest tears are shed. A day when some lucky girl get gorgeous flowers delivered to her job while you suck your teeth because she's got everything you've only read about in fairy tales.

You whine: *Why does she get "nice flowers" compliments all day? We're at work for crying out loud. And why does he have so many pictures of his wife and kids on the desk? It's taking up too much space!*

She boasts: *The night was so wonderful. He took me to my favorite restaurant and then we went to a lovely concert. Tonight, we're taking a walk through Central Park.*

Valentine's Day. A day of love and a day of longing. One is delighted, another is depressed. The eager gentleman is planning his perfect proposal, and you, the lonely waiter, has to bring that "special" dessert with an engagement ring on top. A holiday and a haunting day. A night of melodies and a midnight of melancholy. There's Mickey with Minnie and then there's Curious George with his banana and a blockbuster video. *Sigh*. If everyday were Valentine's Day, the world would be at war over love all year long.

Every year around this time, I go to the store to pick out a few Valentine's Day cards: one for my wife, one for my mom, and one for my sister. I have the routine down pat. This particular V-day, however, I wasn't as prepared as I normally am. I waited until the last minute to purchase my cards, so I'm rushing. I've got dinner on the stove and candles burning back at home. *Shaun. You've got to hurry up. In and out. Don't stop to talk to people about Jesus—nothing. This should only take two minutes.* I race into the store on February 14th. The automated doors swish open. The lady on the loudspeaker announces: "Ladies and Gentleman, the store will be closing in 5 minutes." *I panic. I run. Faster. I'm flustered.* I think to myself, "Why do all store announcers sound like flight attendants nowadays? And why do flight attendants sound like robots...who made up that requi—* "S*haun, not now! You've got no time to analyze the small things."* O.K. Fine. I gather my thoughts and sprint over to the card aisle like a shopper on "Supermarket Sweep." *Great show.* When I finally get there, I see five empty shelves, four birthday cards, three teddy bears, two turtle doves, and a partridge in a heart tree. For real. I mean, there was no partridge, but everything else was pretty accurate. All of the cards were sold out. *Bummer! That's all I need. It's February 14th!* What is a man to do?

I have my moment. I look around for any sign of poetic love. Negative. The only cards remaining are these blank little $1.99 Valentine's Day cards with the white little naked Cupid and the bow and arrow, but I didn't feel like writing a profound message. Besides, I'm buying the card and they want to charge me for the blank space? *Give me a break.* I turn around to walk out of the store, and in bold red letters, I see these words peering down from a really big banner:

"Will YOU Be My Valentine?"

I felt God. It was the scariest thing ever! For a second, it felt like the banner was talking to me. Here I am, in a store on Valentine's day—no card in my hand, no clue what to do next, and this announcement-flight attendant lady screaming into the intercom—and I get that tingly feeling most people only get in church. I sense God's presence. The banner was so striking. I nearly bumped into it and now it was haunting me.

At this point, you think I'm crazy, I'm sure, but someone reading this knows exactly what I'm talking about. It's kind of like that picture you stare at while getting your nails done, and then you look up, and the picture is staring back at you. So you slide to the right and look back quickly, and it's still looking, staring, haunting you! So you shift one more time to the left and bend down four inches and when you look up again, Mona Lisa is still gazing—eye ball to eye ball. Scary, right? Well, that's what this banner seemed to do.

So now, I'm a little freaked out. I say to myself, "Leave, Shaun. Just ignore it." But I don't. I can't. Like the idiotic people we see on scary movies who run up the stairs instead of out of the door, I tiptoe closer toward the banner instead of running away. *Typical.* I read it again...

"Will YOU Be My Valentine?"

I whispered to myself, "Me?" and out of nowhere, I hear some lady in aisle 4 yell, "Yes you!" *My heart stopped beating.* My throat is dry. I swallow hard. Gulp. *Did..that..really...just..happen?* I promise it happened just like that. So now I'm nearly speaking in tongues. I knew she was probably talking to someone else, but the timing of it all convinced me of something far greater than mere coincidence. God was really talking to me! Somehow, someway, God was using that banner and that lady to speak to my heart. But, for what purpose? Was it just about Valentine's Day? Should I have just purchased the $1.99 naked angel card? Of course not. God was trying to get me to write this letter to you...all of you. It was all about evangelism. Step into God's world, readers. This is going to be a fun one.

I AM LOVE

Song of Solomon 2:4 He brought me to the banqueting house, and his banner over me was love.

Below is a letter from God to you. Every time I read it, I feel like God is talking to me all over again. Male or female, God wants to be your Valentine. What will your answer be?

Hey you! Yes you.

I promise I won't take up much of your time. I just had to step into your reality and speak to you, heart to heart. I want you to know that I see you. I hear you. I love you.

For the past few months you've been asking me a lot of questions. It seems like everyone else is living life to the fullest, and here you are, faced with trial after trial after trial. You feel forgotten about. Empty. Lost. If the child isn't misbehaving, then the bills are never-ending. Your job situation is shaky. The lonely nights are overwhelming. You're tired. You're really tired. You are so weighed down sometimes that you can't even find time to cry. I see you. I hear you. I love you.

Above all else, I know you. You know why? Because I made you. I made you before you knew how to make a mistake. I designed you before your mother considered aborting you. I knew you and I know you. You've been hurt so many times. You are tired of the lies, the schemes and the performance. You're at a place in your life where you don't even want a spouse anymore because love has violated you one time too many. You're wishing for authentic love. Understanding. Hope. For one time in your life, you just want to know that this love thing is real. Does that sound about right? If so, keep reading.

Here's the good news: I am Love, with a capital 'L'. Love is My middle name. I am the Love that will never leave you out to dry (Hebrews 13:5).[1] I am the Love that will introduce you to a better way to identify "lower case love." Love is who I am. Everything else outside of Me is imitation. I am Love. I've loved your backside for so long (Psalm 80:3).[2] Would you turn around so I can love your beautiful face? I want a one-on-

one relationship with You. I want to make you smile. I want you to find fulfillment in Me. I want to be in your life to make you better, not worse.

Today, I make a bold step and I ask you ... (nervously because you've rejected me so many times before)...Will YOU be my Valentine? Will you allow me into your heart, once and for all? Will you accept the truth today, this day?

What is the truth? I'm so glad you asked. The truth is, I created you to enjoy life and to never be sad. The truth is that your ancestors (Adam and Eve) chose to eat from a tree that I warned them not to eat from; and ever since, sadness has spread throughout the world like an infectious disease. It's not your fault that you were born like this; which is why I had to do something about it. I sat in heaven and I watched creation's light get dimmer by the second. You all were going in a downward spiral, closer to destruction than you were toward destiny. Creation was going to hell. I couldn't sit there on my throne and do nothing about it. So, I was moved with compassion to step into your universe. I clothed myself in flesh (Philippians 2:8; John 1:14) [3-4] and I was commissioned by my Father to enter the world so that I could become your Valentine. But this love story had a melodramatic twist. I had to die so that you could live (1 Thessalonians 5:9-10). [5] I knew I had to, but I wasn't sprinting toward the cross to do it. I knew they would beat me. I knew they would spit on me. I knew they would mock me. But as I swallowed every whip, every slice, every puncture—oh yeah, they platted a crown of thorns and jammed it on my head (Matthew 27:29) [6]— I thought about you. Yes, you!

I wish I could tell you I felt every slash, but the truth is, I didn't. I was so distracted by your face inside of that invisible frame. Before I knew it, they had drilled a few nails into my hands (John 20:25) [7] and I was pinned to a cross like a thumbtack pressed up against a wooden bulletin board. I had a bird's eye view of persecution, but I had a Love's eye view of forgiveness.

I gave up my life (they didn't kill me-John 10:18), [8] but obviously I'm not dead if I'm writing to you now. Wanna know what happened? I died and on the third day, I resurrected (1 Corinthians 15:3-4). [9] After I rose, I walked around to show some people what had happened, and then after a few weeks, I returned back to heaven.

I don't want to bore you, (I tend to ramble when I'm nervous) so let me just cut to the chase: I want you to be mine forever. I want to marry you, and bring you up to my Father's house so that we can be one (John 14:2). [10]

But before we get married, I've got to be in relationship with you. I don't want another bad relationship to have control over you. I want to love you, and guide you, and help you. That framed picture I saw 2,000 years ago during my field trip to earth, that was nice; but I want to meet you face to face. The only way that can happen is if you give me a chance. Let go of those old clothes, believe in me, and then join me and the angels for a cup of tea after your life audition is over (John 14:1).[11]

Would you be my Valentine....please? Circle YES or NO.

-If you circled YES

YAAAAAAAAY! Me and the angels are partyinnnnnnn' right now in heaven. If you said yes and if you've realized in your heart of hearts that you want to be cleansed from the dirty sins life has accumulated, all you have to do is open your arms and get ready for me to fill you with more love. If you believe in me, and if you believe I am a Forgiver, then ask for forgiveness (Ephesians 1:7).[12] And if you believe that I actually came down to earth, died, and rose, then you qualify for instant salvation and security through me. You are what church people call "saved" (Romans 10:9-10).[13] I call it "loving you with a tighter grip" because I have always loved you, even when you didn't love Me. The difference now is that you'll actually *feel* My love and you'll know in a more intimate way the One from whom this love comes.

-If you circled NO

My heart is broken. I've been rejected again. I will not be satisfied until I win your love. So I will steadily knock at the door of your heart, and listen closely for you to respond. If ever you have a change of heart, I will gladly accept you. On Valentine's Day or not.

P.S.--There's so much more I wish I could tell you. But for now, just know that I love you.

Agape,

J.C.

------------ ◈ ------------

Prayer of Salvation: Savior, I believe. I believe You died for my sins, rose with all power, and You have given me the power to do greater works than You (John 14:12). 14 I ask for Your forgiveness. I pray for Your insight. Make me sensitive to Your words. Lead me to a community of believers who can help me in this journey. Teach me how to love. In the name of the One whose banner over me is Love, Amen.

------------ ◈ ------------

As Simple as "THAT"

John 3:16,17 For God so loved the world that he gave his only begotten Son, that whosoever believeth in him should not perish, but have everlasting life. For God sent not his Son into the world to condemn the world; but that the world through him might be saved.

God loves us so much *that* He gave His only begotten Son.
God loves us so much *that* He gave His only.
God loves us so much *that* He gave.
God loves us so much *that.*
That.

Can I just stop right here and talk about the 'that' in John 3:16? It is, I think, the most powerful word in this verse because it reveals why God is not like us humans. You see, humans have a beautiful way of making cute promises without following through. We tell our loved ones that we love them and we tell them how difficult life would be without them. We make vows to nurse them if they are sick and save them from the violent waves if they are drowning. Our promises are really poetic, but they lack proof. You say out of your mouth that you will jump from the top of the highest mountain and you will crawl through the darkest cave, but how do I truly know you will keep your word? Unlike us, God showed us His love by giving "that" proof to His poetic promise. He showed us through His "that" act how spoken promises can become living proof once poetry becomes more than pretty words on a piece of a paper. It wasn't enough for God to simply stand back from a distance and love the world. He was moved with compassion and stepped into our chaos (Matthew 9:36).[15] He motioned toward us before we could ever know to turn toward Him (Romans 5:8).[16] This is why "that" is so important in John 3:16. It is evidence of Love's willingness to win us back from the slavery of sin (Romans 6:2-4).[17] Everything after

> ------------◈------------
> *Prayer: Lord, You have called us as Christians to give, and not only to give, but to sacrifice. Allow me to give more than I take, receive less than I contribute, and say "no" to those things I really don't need. Amen*
> ------------◈------------

"that" shows evidence of God's love for us: He gave us His only begotten son, He gave us the gift of faith (belief), and He gave us everlasting life. So here's some advice for every reader. If you want people to believe your promises, turn your "I will do" into a "that I gave" statement. Many people will try to tell you they love you and many dead-beat partners, for example, will promise to get a job eventually. That's really poetic. But when your home is nearing foreclosure and you are slaving to keep food on the table, you need to see some "thats" or you're going to have to find another "this!" It's as simple as "that."

WORD OF ADVICE FOR THE YOUNG LADIES

Let me take a momentary detour to offer a brief word of wisdom for the young ladies reading. Ladies, don't waste your value and worth chasing after a man who doesn't do "that," "this" or anything in between. He doesn't work. He doesn't pray. He doesn't clean. He doesn't church. You pay the bills. You clean the house. You bail him out time and time again. You're steadily hoping he will change, and instead of getting better, he gets worse.

In my opinion, you need to give him a nice wave offering, seal it with a goodbye, and on the way out, point him to the word "that" in John 3:16. Literally find a bright yellow highlighter and circle "that." Then, leave him to figure out what it means. After he comes back to you (because you will not go back to him), he will be confused and disoriented. You tell him with as much tenacity as you can muster up: "Listen. I am God's daughter. God gave His very best for me. God loved me so much "that." And because of His *that*, I won't take *this*. I can't allow the worst in you to produce the fair in me. I can't settle for anything less than the best because I've got the best in Him. The Lord bless you and keep you, and may His face shine upon you. Goodbye! (Numbers 6:24-25)"[18] I know it might be difficult to do this. I realize that you are in love with love, but if what he is giving you is less than God's best, you need to move on. It will only hurt more and more as you vow to give your all, and he struggles to give ten percent. Don't let a man treat you like a tithe. If he doesn't see your earthly value, then he definitely can't handle your spiritual worth.

Prayer: Righteous Judge, for the abused as well as the abuser, I pray your hand of protection and your hand of correction. Chasten out our desires to find complacency in abuse. Give us the strength to leave hostile environments. Introduce us to Love with a capital L. In Christ's Name. Amen

I say this because I have witnessed firsthand the effects of love abuse. And I am so very tired of innocent women (and men) getting abused and mistreated (both in the body of Christ and outside of it). I am tired of hearing stories about the woman who is mistreated by a man who never loved her, all because she couldn't see her inner value and strength. Rarely does the narrative change. She finally gets out of a bad relationship and finds comfort in a new one. Then, three months later, the same thing is happening again. And instead of blaming him, she blames herself. Something is just not right with this picture.

Ladies, here is a two-fold mirror for you to consider. Once you truly see your worth, a man will notice how seriously you take your relationship with God. And once you take your relationship with God seriously, a man will see your true worth. Pardon the double negative, but don't compromise for nobody! You don't have to beg anyone to love you. You don't have to settle for a man on the 50% off Clearance rack! Walk away and don't look back. You've already got perfect love from the God "that" gave in John 3:16. Women are twenty times more attractive when they don't appear desperate. Your favor rate goes up when you allow the beam of God's faith-light to shine through you. So, let it shine! Let it shine! Let it shine! And everything that ruins your shine, let it go, let it go, let it go!

GOD'S LOVE FOR CREATION WAS CONFIRMED WHEN HE GAVE HIS ONLY BEGOTTEN SON

Now, back to our regular programming. God confirmed His Love for us when He gave up His only Son. He sent us a confirmation number while we were yet sinners. You do know what a confirmation number is, right? If not, let me explain. When someone pays a bill, there is a number that comes to your inbox or you hear it over the phone. The operator will say something like, "This message confirms your payment to _____ in the amount of _____." But check this. Even before the money is debited from the account, you receive a confirmation number. And this confirmation number is important because it protects you from overcharge. That is, if the bill collector tries to charge you again for a debt already paid, the confirmation number will speak for you and will help alleviate a double charge. Well aren't you glad that God consolidated our worldly debt problem by making one final sacrificial payment? Aren't you glad that Jesus issued you a confirmation number to which you can always refer (in John 3:16)[19] as your receipt of payment? I sure am.

This is very important for us to understand so I will reiterate it here. John 3:16 teaches us that God sent His only Son as the confirmation number into our worldly account and now we have access to the Father through Him. Ephesians 2:18 makes it clear: "For through him we both have access by one Spirit unto the Father." That means, we have both abundant life and everlasting life because of Jesus! God didn't allow the penalty price of sin (death-Romans 6:23)[20] to debit our account. He assumed our debts even while we were still charging sin to our worldly account. He confirmed our payment by serving as the Ultimate sacrifice and, as that sacrifice, His blood sealed our salvation (Romans 3:25; Romans 5:11).[21-22] Jesus didn't wait for a reply to all. He didn't require my signature. He simply said, "Yes, they are worth it all. Charge their sins to me!" And in just one clean swipe, the whole world was given access into life everlasting. God so loved the world "that!"

I hope you see my point by now. Love is not love until you show it. You've got to show some form of confirmation that indicates the depth of your love. How else will I know that you love what you say you love? I need a "that." You're only bluffing and twisting my leg if you say you love me, but you never do anything to show me. God's love for me was confirmed when He gave. God did not bluff or renege on His promise. He loved us so much "that." So, before we shout about what He gave and before we bask in the purpose of the gift He gave, we need to just be thankful *that* He gave.

DON'T PUT AN EXPIRATION DATE ON JOHN 3:16

For *that* reason, every Christian should feel something special when reading John 3:16. We should feel revived, renewed, and reminded. But sadly, I don't think we feel much anymore. I think Scriptures like Psalm 23, Genesis 1:1, and John 3:16 are on back order in our "give me a new word" churches. These Scriptures seem to have reached their expiration date and now, if we decide to preach a sermon, one of the last places we will ever think to go is John 3:16. This is a problem. Primarily because we end up treating the Holy Book like a lottery ticket—we can't play the same numbers the same way.

Instead, we've got to spice it up a little and change some things around to satisfy our own selfish desires. Besides, this might be the day that someone hears our great sermon and pays us for our masterful work. Or, this could be the day when they buy my book, not because God told me to write it, but because I needed a gig to make me a holy superstar. What are we doing? We open the Bible as if we are going on a treasure hunt to find a new piece of gold, and sometimes we pass right over the valley of precious revelation in search for a nugget of human argumentation. What we search for in Scripture must not bring more attention to the reader than it does the Writer.

------------◈------------

Prayer: Forgive me for trying to be spectacular. As one writer put it, "Make me invisible." Help me not to see myself in anything I do for thee. Help me to see You in all that I do. Help me to be as shocked as the reader or hearer of the Word is, at the sound of your voice through me. Amen.

------------◈------------

WHAT IT MEANS TO BE LOVED BY GOD

In closing, let us bask in the love of God for a moment. Let's meditate on the love God has revealed to us through Jesus and let us give thanks for the sacrifice of our Lord and Savior. As I sit down to consider the extent of God's love, I am ushered into the courts of repentance. I am brought low into the basement of humility. The towering twins of grace and mercy shadow me. The beauty of God's holiness blinds me. I forget to remember the pain I once felt. This is what it means to be loved by God. I am given a raincoat to protect me from the storms of life. The abuse I once endured slowly fades away. I am loved by God and I am in love with God. This is what it means to be loved by Compassion himself.

To be loved by God is to always be on the mind of the Creator. To be loved by God is to be accepted into the fellowship of divine friendship. To be loved by God is to be liked by God. Whether you know it or not, your entire life will change when you fall in love with Jesus. One touch from God's love garment will heal the hurts of yesterday. One taste of God's homemade love soup will leave you hungry for more. One word from the mouth of God will inspire you to want to know the heart of God. This is what it means to be loved by God.

I challenge you to take a moment to reread John 3:16 today. Get a "that" revelation. Get lost in the sand and sea of the heavenly beach called "that." Dive headfirst into the waters with the fish, and realize, *"God you loved me so much that you created the fish just for me, and me just for the fish. You created the crab so that this little mermaid could have a friend under the sea."* Get on an airplane, and fly into the clouds and realize, *"God you loved me so much that you never let it rain above the clouds!"* John 3:16 should remain on the front burner of every Christian's mental oven. Don't let it expire; for the ingredients in John 3:16 keep the spices of Christian living fresh and the oils of Christian dying ablaze. Stir the Scriptures on a daily basis. Taste something new. Never let the love of God go stale in your mind. Don't discount the power, promise, and potential of Jesus Christ. God so loved the world "that." And because "that" kind of love was extended toward us, we have an obligation as a Christian community to tag "that" love onto others.

Let's get to the heart of the soul and not just the surface of the mind. Let's dare to launch out into the deep for the sake of a sinking ship. Let's become in sync with what the spirit of God is saying to the church. Let's take our foot off the brakes and just learn to trust God. Love God with all of your being and remember God loves you dearly. The moment we forget what it means to be loved by God is the moment we settle for less than what God has promised.

------------◇------------

Prayer: Compassion, Your love has changed my life. Your example has challenged me to become a better person. I acknowledge today that You are the True and Living Love Gift. You are the source from which love comes. You are the Lover of my Soul. Transform me, I pray, into a loving vessel, that I might demonstrate Your love to an unhealthy generation. To a people who are searching for love in all of the wrong places, help me not to judge. Help me, rather, to be an example to those who may never set foot in a church. I love You and I thank You for "that" sacrifice. In Christ's name. Amen

------------◇------------

Questions for Introspection

1) Powerful revelations are sometimes hidden in the smallest word or in the biggest banner. How many "banners" have you passed by this week? Is God using anything extraordinary to speak to you about the ordinary? If so, name it. Discuss it. Write about it.

2) Once the church internalizes John 3:16 and begins to imagine the depths of simple words like "that," it will change how we view preaching. How many times have you read John 3:16 and decided to reflect on nothing more than the word "that" or "for" or "only?" Reread this verse with new eyes. What word(s) stick out to you? Why?

Practical Points

1

To be loved by God is to be loved by the absolute best. Will you be God's Valentine? God loves you so much *that* He gave His only and His every at the same time. He's already confirmed His love. Don't be afraid to love God back. God won't bite. He didn't come into the world to condemn you. Just love Him back (Romans 8:1).[23]

2

Preachers and teachers, never feel intimidated or pressured into living up to the expectations and regulations of man. God has called you and God will use others to shape that call, but ultimately, it is God who will empower you to share the good news in a great and unique way.

3

As beneficiaries of Christ's love, we must always be prepared to show the love of God to a dying world (Romans 5:5).[24] It is our responsibility to live out John 3:16. There are many people out there looking for a trace of God's love. Allow your light to shine in ways that cause men to ask, "What must I do to be saved? (Acts 16:30)"[25] Let your embrace, your emails, your conversations always point up to Jesus, and not inward toward your self. It is in Him that we live, move, and have our being (Acts 17:28).[26]

4

Love takes on a different form once you fall in love with Jesus. When discerning about a life partner, be sure that she or he takes Love (with a capital L) seriously. *Love* is major, money is minor. *Love* is major, looks are minor. Don't major on a minor. See your future spouse from Love's perspective before you end up simply tolerating someone who looks the part, but doesn't live the Love.

5 Whenever you are in worship and you need an image to think about, I strongly suggest thinking of the cross. But remember, Jesus is no longer there. Picture the pain and agony of a Man, like you and me, giving himself for us. Picture the blood streaming down and the soft whispers like "Father, forgive them," or "It is finished." See the cross and the tomb. Empty. No evidence or trace of Jesus because He now sits on the throne, (Revelations 3:21)[27] interceding constantly for us (Romans 8:34),[28] believing with us, forgiving us (Ephesians 1:6-7).[29]

Scripture Glossary

[1]**Hebrews 13:5** *Let your conversation be without covetousness; and be content with such things as ye have: for he hath said, I will never leave thee, nor forsake thee.*

[2]**Psalm 80:3** *Turn us again, O God, and cause thy face to shine; and we shall be saved.*

[3]**Philippians 2:8** *And being found in fashion as a man, he humbled himself, and became obedient unto death, even the death of the cross.*

[4]**John 1:14** *And the Word was made flesh, and dwelt among us, (and we beheld his glory, the glory as of the only begotten of the Father,) full of grace and truth.*

[5]**1 Thessalonians 5:9-10** *For God hath not appointed us to wrath, but to obtain salvation by our Lord Jesus Christ, Who died for us, that, whether we wake or sleep, we should live together with him.*

[6]**Matthew 27:29** *And when they had platted a crown of thorns, they put it upon his head, and a reed in his right hand: and they bowed the knee before him, and mocked him, saying, Hail, King of*

the Jews!

[7]**John 20:25** *The other disciples therefore said unto him, We have seen the LORD. But he said unto them, Except I shall see in his hands the print of the nails, and put my finger into the print of the nails, and thrust my hand into his side, I will not believe.*

[8]**John 10:18** *No man taketh it from me, but I lay it down of myself. I have power to lay it down, and I have power to take it again. This commandment have I received of my Father.*

[9]**1 Corinthians 15:3-4** *For I delivered unto you first of all that which I also received, how that Christ died for our sins according to the scriptures; And that he was buried, and that he rose again the third day according to the scriptures.*

[10]**John 14:2** *In my Father's house are many mansions: if it were not so, I would have told you. I go to prepare a place for you.*

[11]**John 14:1** *Let not your heart be troubled: ye believe in God, believe also in me.*

[12]**Ephesians 1:7** *In whom we have redemption through his blood, the forgiveness of sins, according to the riches of his grace.*

[13]**Romans 10:9-10** *That if thou shalt confess with thy mouth the Lord Jesus, and shalt believe in thine heart that God hath raised him from the dead, thou shalt be saved. For with the heart man believeth unto righteousness; and with the mouth confession is made unto salvation.*

[14]**John 14:12** *Verily, verily, I say unto you, He that believeth on me, the works that I do shall he do also; and greater works than these shall he do; because I go unto my Father.*

[15]**Matthew 9:36** *But when he saw the multitudes, he was moved with compassion on them, because they fainted, and were scattered abroad, as sheep having no shepherd.*

¹⁶**Romans 5:8** *But God commendeth his love toward us, in that, while we were yet sinners, Christ died for us.*

¹⁷**Romans 6:2-4** *God forbid. How shall we, that are dead to sin, live any longer therein? Know ye not, that so many of us as were baptized into Jesus Christ were baptized into his death? Therefore we are buried with him by baptism into death: that like as Christ was raised up from the dead by the glory of the Father, even so we also should walk in newness of life.*

¹⁸**Numbers 6:24-25** *The LORD bless thee, and keep thee: The LORD make his face shine upon thee, and be gracious unto thee.*

¹⁹**John 3:16** *For God so loved the world, that he gave his only begotten Son, that whosoever believeth in him should not perish, but have everlasting life.*

²⁰**Romans 6:23** *For the wages of sin is death; but the gift of God is eternal life through Jesus Christ our Lord.*

²¹**Romans 3:25** *Whom God hath set forth to be a propitiation through faith in his blood, to declare his righteousness for the remission of sins that are past, through the forbearance of God.*

²²**Romans 5:11** *And not only so, but we also joy in God through our Lord Jesus Christ, by whom we have now received the atonement.*

²³**Romans 8:1** *There is therefore now no condemnation to them which are in Christ Jesus, who walk not after the flesh, but after the Spirit.*

²⁴**Romans 5:5** *And hope maketh not ashamed; because the love of God is shed abroad in our hearts by the Holy Ghost which is given unto us.*

²⁵**Acts 16:30** *And brought them out, and said, Sirs, what must I do to be saved?*

[26]**Acts 17:28** *For in him we live, and move, and have our being; as certain also of your own poets have said, For we are also his offspring.*

[27]**Revelation 3:21** *To him that overcometh will I grant to sit with me in my throne, even as I also overcame, and am set down with my Father in his throne.*

[28]**Romans 8:38** *Who is he that condemneth? It is Christ that died, yea rather, that is risen again, who is even at the right hand of God, who also maketh intercession for us.*

[29]**Ephesians 1:6-7** *To the praise of the glory of his grace, wherein he hath made us accepted in the beloved. In whom we have redemption through his blood, the forgiveness of sins, according to the riches of his grace.*

AFTERWORD

You have reached the end of this journey. Congratulations! Now, please, please, pretty please... go and write your own chronicles. Consider others around you and take note of God's voice everywhere. Write until you can't write anymore, and then read what you've written if you find yourself discouraged, clueless, or torn between one decision and the next. Pull all of your little notes together and formulate a book. You never know how your perspective on any given subject will bring clarity and transformation to someone else.

I hope these chronicles have inspired you to be used by God as well.

Be Blessed! —Shaun

ACKNOWLEDGMENTS

If it takes a community to raise a child, then surely it took a country to produce this book. All of my appreciation goes to Jesus Christ, first and foremost, for His everlasting faithfulness and continued grace. God, I thank You for allowing me to hear Pastor Sheryl Brady's sermon "Spirit of a Finisher." I thank You for introducing me to Ron Hutchcraft Ministries five years ago (please visit his website if you've never heard of him). I thank You for breathing through me and believing for me when I lost faith in myself. Even when I dropped the ball, you whispered encouragement to me from someone else; and that is how this book got completed.

There are hosts of people for whom I am especially grateful as well. To my father, Louis Saunders, thank you for instilling in me the gift to teach. You have been a living example of the effect dedicated teaching will have on generations of children unborn. For my mom, "Sis. Debra," who knows me better than I know myself. Thank you for speaking life—always and forever! To my step-dad, "Minister Mike," thank you for living the life—always and forever! To my baby sister, Charla, thank you for being the best sister a brother could ever have! You don't know this, but whenever I got frustrated and whenever I said, "I'm done, I'm not writing anymore," it was your face I saw, cheering me on and encouraging me to finish this book! Know that I wrote this book with you in mind. And when I finished it, I said, "If no one else likes it, at least my sister will be my biggest fan."

And to my editors: Rev. CJ Rhodes, Minister Lyvonne Briggs, Bro. Christopher Brown, and Pastor Boris Bayless. I'm sure you all have had pleasure in reading five thousand varying drafts of the same chronicle, only for me to send an updated one within minutes of you reading the last one I sent! I'm crazy, I know. But all of the editorial suggestions, revisions, and assistance has helped me to imagine this book as an effective resource for communities much larger than I can see right now. Thank you all for believing in me. You'll never know how much your smiley faces (CJ), your poetic elegance (Boris), your profound email confessions (Lyvonne,) and your "I believe in you's" (Chris) have meant to me! Thank you. To Danny Mercedes, thank you for conceptualizing the book cover. I envisioned it, you designed it!

And to all of my sponsors and close friends: Most people do not know this, but I reached out to a few hundred people, asking for assistance with the production of this book. 30 people (and families) responded. Their names are:

Charla Saunders, Dr. Maurice Wallace, Pamela Wallace, Lucy Watson, The Tucker Family, Delores Downing, Hattie Hamilton, Willie Hamilton, Pastor Coleman and family, Pastor Boris and Theresa Bayless, Kirk Johnson, Braxton Shelley, HPC Daycare Staff, Matt Rose, Debra Wyatt, Sandra Bumpass, Wendy Ekua Quansah, Patricia Hutchins, George Smith, Tamara Lawrence, Barbara Ecton, Oluwatomisin Oredein, Mommy, Michael Przybylko, Ashley Martin, Dr. Cassandra Autry, Shaneah Taylor, Darnell Moore, Mary McMullen and Tolu Sosanya.

Not only will your names be forever archived in this book, but God will forever remember you for sowing into this embryonic project. Thank you! Thank you! Thank you! Believe me when I say: this book could not have been printed and disseminated without you. Every time I received a donation notification, I was assured, "Somebody believes in the dream in me." Yet, you never read a single chapter; you never asked for an in-depth breakdown. You simply sowed into my dream, and because of you, this has come to pass. Thank you. My heart is overwhelmed with joy. I pray you will continue to support our hopeful endeavors.

And to my spiritual leaders: I have a team of folks who have been mega-important to my spiritual upbringing. My brother, Elder Shaheed Hamilton, has taught me perseverance and dedication. My sister-in-law Fee has taught me the power of prayer and the importance of spiritual sensitivity to the Spirit of God. My mother in the Gospel, Elder Johnnie Mae Smith, has taught me faithfulness and dedication (especially when no one sees you). My big sis, Elder Fondrea Lewis, has taught me how to appreciate my uniqueness and flourish in the midst of famine. My other "sister", Shanny, has taught me how powerful support from the sidelines can be. My Fayetteville mom, Apostle Carolyn Hicks, introduced me to international ministry and anointed this project long before its completion. And Jade, those text messages and emails were always on time.

My pastor from Durham, NC, Dr. Maurice Wallace, has served as a teaching mentor, a true friend, and an exemplary witness at Duke University. Doc, thank you for giving me the space to grow, for allowing me to be creative, and for affirming my gift when very few people in North Carolina understood anything about me. Pam Wallace, thank you for caring. You have redefined that word for me. And to Pastor Damarcus Johnson and Lady Amy Johnson, thank you for praying for me. I am sure many people can teach on prayer, but I am not convinced that many people actually pray. For you two, I am beyond sure. I have felt your prayers, I have received your words of encouragement and caution, and no, it's not a lieutenant! (personal joke ☺)

And to Bishop Carolyn Webb, Presiding Prelate of the New Dimensions Worldwide Ministries – I never had a chance to speak to you before the book's completion, but every time I prayed about the title I would hear you scream, "You've got to SEE GOD!" And I knew I would keep the title as simple and as thought-provoking as it is. Thank you for being a pillar of wisdom, a beacon of light, a testimony of hope, and a cheerful, encouraging and "touchable" leader. Your crown in heaven is great! I love you!

To my Seton Hall crew, Substance praise and worship team, and a host of other friends who have asked me 1,000 times "When is the book coming out?" I've got news for you! It's done! It's written! It is finished! Now, on to volume 2! Love you all.

And last but not least, to the woman who makes my heart sing off key. To my visible strength who stands beside me, cries with me, laughs with me, and puts up with my silent spells; to the queen of my heart, to the love of my life. Ana, I owe all of this to you. I don't think "Thank You" will adequately convey what I wish to say, but "thank you" multiplied by one million might touch the iceberg. Not only did you assist me with formatting this book, finalizing the book cover, updating and redesigning the website, sending emails and creating images for Godzchild, but you have ministered to my brokenness; you have labored tirelessly with me, you have put up with my meticulousness, and you're still pushing me to believe that I can do all things through Christ which is our strength. You epitomize what it means to be a helpmate. I love you. I like you. I'm grateful to serve you as your husband. God gave me His best when He gave me you. I have no desire for anything else.

GODZCHILD PUBLICATIONS

Have a story to tell?

Has God given you ideas for a book or a play but you have no clue where to begin?

Do you have an eager desire to finish what you've started?

If you answered "YES" to any of these questions, perhaps Godzchild, Inc. can assist you!

Godzchild, Inc. seeks to win souls and edify the Kingdom of God through the ministries of publication and performance.

Godzchild Publications, a division of Godzchild, Inc., endeavors to serve as a platform for "untrained" preachers and teachers (academically, institutionally or otherwise). We want to ensure that your God-given message is heard, transcribed, packaged, printed and disseminated. We are committed to your vision and we believe in the God in you!

Our Services Include:

"Holy Ghost" Writing and Manuscript Editing
Performing Arts Workshops and Vocal Arrangements
Church Conference Plays/Skits
Production Management
Writing Consultations/Seminars
College and Scholarship Assistantship

Visit www.godzchildproductions.net today!
God has great things in store for us!

We live to serve God, and we'd love to serve you.
For booking information and other requests, contact (973) 699-1107

......Coming Soon......

WE Must, WE Shall:
The Worship and Evangelism Workbook
൚

Seeing God In Everything
Volume II
൚

Advice 4 Babes in Christ:
An ABC Guide to Life after Salvation
൚